M000203615

WINE

A BEGINNER'S GUIDE

WINE
A BEGINNER'S GUIDE

BY KEN FREDRICKSON
Master Sommelier

ROCKRIDGE
PRESS

Interior and Cover Designer: Amanda Kirk
Art Producer: Michael Hardgrove
Editor: Sean Newcott
Production Editor: Jenna Dutton

Illustration © Ryn Frank, 2019.

Photography © Lido Vannucchi, pp. v, vi, xii, 4, 8, 10, 26, 34, 70, 88, 112, 122, 128, 146; StockFood/PhotoCuisine/Hubert Taillard, p. ii; Stocksy/ Jill Chen, p. 19; Shutterstock/Brent Hofackere, p. 24; Stocksy/Gillian Vann, p. 54; Getty Images/mphillips007, p. 85; Stockfood/Jennifer Martin, p. 120. Flags © Shutterstock/admin_design.

Author photos courtesy of © Zachera Wollenberg

ISBN: Print 978-1-64611-054-4 | eBook 978-1-64611-055-1

R0

**FOR MY
FOUR-YEAR-OLD
SON, ALESSANDRO:**
*You are my compass,
and the joyful
embodiment of
future promise.*

Vineyards in late September, ready for the harvest.

CONTENTS

Foreword viii Introduction x

—

CHAPTER ONE
Wine 101 1

CHAPTER TWO
Wine Builds Character 27

CHAPTER THREE
Style and Substance 35

CHAPTER FOUR
How to Taste Wine 55

CHAPTER FIVE
Handle Wine Like
a Sommelier 71

CHAPTER SIX
Wine Around the World 89

CHAPTER SEVEN
Pairing Wine with Food 123

—

Conclusion 137 Resources 138 Index 140

FOREWORD

I **MET KEN FREDRICKSON A DOZEN YEARS AGO;**
with our mutual respect for our craft, a shared love
of bicycles and the Blackhawks hockey team, and, of
course, wine, our friendship was immediate.

My father, Bobby, owned a smokehouse and delicatessen
where, as a child, I worked weekends and school breaks
alongside him. The tasks were varied and some days were
filled with less-than-glamorous projects, such as pulling
heavy fish from brine solution and hanging them in the
smokehouse. This childhood experience didn't just earn
me some spending money; it laid the foundation that food
could be a "life discovery" vehicle.

When my partners and I opened Blackbird, our first
restaurant, our vision was to create a complete dining experience. This meant developing a well-written, concise wine
list in complete harmony with the philosophy of the food:
We wanted flavors that were sophisticated, yet comfortable
and approachable. Tasting with limited (but quickly bur-
geoning) knowledge was an exercise in honesty—there was
no brand influence, no long-term history, and no intellectual constraint. Working through this opening process was
when I realized wine could be—and should be—an integral
part of the dining experience. I mean, why not? If we were
pushing hard to cook and eat delicious, then of course
we should drink delicious, too. From that point on, we

realized the important role of the wine director/sommelier in our restaurants, and we continue to place a great deal of emphasis on beverage, both for our staff and our guests.

Although Ken has never worked for One Off Hospitality directly, for many years he has worked with us and alongside us, offering unwavering support through customer service, education, charitable giving, and, of course, wickedly great wine selections.

It is just so much fun to taste wine and food with Ken. So. Much. Fun. It's an all-senses, completely engaging experience: His ease in explaining complicated subjects, his passionate appreciation of flavors, and his endless quest for amusement are, frankly, unsurpassed. Honestly, for many years, in the back of my mind, I was selfishly hoping he would someday write a book like this.

That day is here.

This book will serve so many in an endless variety of ways: It provides excellent general knowledge, great tips for party planning, clarification of geeky wine vernacular, and insights into how to enjoy wine more fully—all wrapped in a grateful, energetic, and joyful package.

I couldn't be more thrilled that he's publishing this incomparable beginner's guide to wine. It's unpretentious, approachable, funny, and generous—a lot like Ken.

Chef Paul Kahan

INTRODUCTION

WINE WASN'T PART OF THE CULTURE IN OUR conservative, rural-Idaho family, so my first serious introduction to wine happened serendipitously.

After growing up on a working ranch, I attended the University of Nevada, Las Vegas, William F. Harrah College of Hospitality with visions of becoming a hotel manager. With UNLV's program established as my academic curriculum, I had to figure out my equally important social one. UNLV's campus Wine Club was just starting and was attempting to build membership with a compelling pitch: "Drink wine and meet people." I signed up immediately.

Little did I know that my ranch upbringing would gift me with a conditioned sense of smell and a plethora of wine descriptors. Nosing my very first older Bordeaux, I quickly identified and rattled off the familiar aromas of wood shavings, worn saddle leather, and manure—that glass of wine brought the sense memories rushing back. And I was hooked.

I never imagined I would go on to work with some of the greatest American chefs, including Charlie Trotter and Wolfgang Puck. But it was all of these experiences, cumulatively, that allowed me to earn the Master Sommelier Diploma before the age of 30.

I have owned restaurants, wine bars, retail shops, and even a winery; around every corner another incredible opportunity and challenge beckoned. I realized the subject

of wine was truly infinite: ever-changing, vast in its scope, and exactly what I loved.

In 2003, I returned to UNLV as an adjunct professor teaching Wine Appreciation. One obstacle in teaching the course was that I could not find a solid introductory level book as a reference guide. You now hold that book in your hands. An all-inclusive, introductory-level reference guide to the world of wine, it covers wine regions, wine styles, grape varieties, tasting, storing, and serving wine. It's filled with tips, tricks, current trends, and personal insights. These pages will expose you to a sincere view of a beloved industry that fosters and celebrates curiosity, cultural exploration, and world travel.

This book distills an enormous amount of information down to the bare necessities in order to build vocabulary and provide direction. If you spend just a few minutes a day reading it—even skimming—while sipping a glass, you will be adequately versed about wine from a master sommelier's perspective. Ultimately, I hope it will help guide you to what you love to drink. But who knows? You may find yourself working on the floor of a fine dining restaurant as a sommelier. At the very least, you'll soon host the best and most lively wine parties in the neighborhood.

Santé!

Ken Fredrickson, Master Sommelier

Perfectly ripened
grapes on double
Cordon vines.

1

WINE 101

Learning about wine is deliciously interdisciplinary. There's lots of science (chemistry, biology, botany, geology) as well as culture, history, and mythology. There are maps to pore over and, if you're lucky, lands to discover. Best of all, there are flavors, textures, and aromas to stir your soul. If you've been bitten by the wine bug, like I have, wine isn't merely sensory, but intellectual; as your knowledge of wine deepens, so will your enjoyment of it. So let's start with the basics: What is that shimmering liquid in your glass and how is it made?

WINEMAKING FROM VINEYARD TO BOTTLE

STEP 1

Harvest

One adage you'll hear a lot is "great wine is made in the vineyard." It's cliché, but nonetheless true. Wine is fermented grape juice, so if the grapes aren't good, the wine won't be either. All sorts of pruning, training, leaf trimming, plowing, fertilizing, and other year-round vineyard work leads to a moment, usually between August and October (between February and April in the Southern Hemisphere), when ripe grapes are harvested to be made into wine. Different varieties mature at different paces, so depending on the size of the operation, harvest can stretch over several months.

Choosing when to harvest is a big moment and can make the difference between a good grape and a not-so-good one. Vintners walk their vineyards and taste grapes to determine when to harvest; most analyze sugar concentrations and pH levels to arrive at a specific date.

Once the grower or winemaker decides to pick, it's go time. Just as a peach on your kitchen counter may be just okay today and fantastic tomorrow, the timing here is essential. One hot day can cause an unwanted jump in sugars. Wine grapes are so sensitive to temperature that growers sometimes harvest in the middle of the night, when it's coolest.

Hand-harvested
grapes are placed
in small bins.

"The Crush"

Once the harvested grapes arrive at the winery, the messy work of destemming, crushing, and pressing them begins. You've seen images of country folk locking arms and traipsing around a wooden vat, stomping grapes with their feet, right? Some people still do that. Most, however, pour the bunches into a mechanical destemmer/crusher, which removes the stems and crushes the grapes, which are then pumped or otherwise transferred into the vessel where they'll be fermented.

White and red grapes are (usually) treated differently: White grapes are not just destemmed and crushed, but also pressed—meaning that the juice is extracted from the slurry of skins, seeds, and pulp with a press. The idea is to separate juice from solids before fermentation.

By contrast, red grapes are crushed and their skins, seeds—and, occasionally, stems—macerate in the juice. The juice in the grapes starts out clear; it obtains color from anthocyanins in the skins, while also extracting tannins and other flavor compounds from the solids. Whether white or red, the crushed/pressed juice that is about to become wine is called must.

Fermentation

Fermentation is when yeast metabolizes sugar (glucose, fructose) and creates roughly equal amounts of ethyl alcohol and carbon dioxide (CO_2). If you've ever made homemade pizza dough, the start of a wine fermentation will sound familiar: It begins by activating yeast, often from a package. In some cases, winemakers let the fermentation occur spontaneously, using only the ambient, or "wild," yeasts that have collected in the winery and on the grapes. This is riskier (and slower) than inoculating the must with a cultured yeast. Otherwise, winemakers have countless commercial cultured yeast strains to choose from, each yielding a different flavor and aroma compound in the wine.

When the must hasn't yet started fermenting, winemakers carefully monitor its exposure to oxygen. Because red wine must contains antioxidants from its contact with the skins, it's more inured against exposure to air than the pressed-off white grape juice, which is often transferred to a sealed vessel to keep oxygen out. Like an apple that begins to brown after it's cut in half, the must is similarly susceptible to oxygen. In both the fermentation and aging processes, oxygen is friend (when exposure is incremental) and foe (when it's excessive).

After yeast is added to the must, the mixture starts bubbling away as yeast devours sugar and creates ethanol/CO_2 as by-products (the latter helping stave off oxidation). The more sugar in the juice, the more alcohol in the wine, and there are hundreds of other biochemical compounds produced during fermentation that shape the flavor, aroma, and texture of the wine. These compounds (esters, aldehydes, glycerol, fatty acids, thiols—the list goes on) number in the hundreds but collectively account for only a tiny fraction of the chemical composition of a finished bottle of wine, which is still, despite everything, more than 80 percent water.

During red wine fermentation, the CO_2 gas pushes the skins and other solids to the top of the tank, forming a "cap" of skins atop the juice; winemakers—to reintroduce the solids into the juice to extract more

Breaking up the grape "cap" during fermentation, also called "punching down the cap."

flavor/color—either punch down those skins with a plunger or pump the juice out of the bottom of the tank and spray it over the mass of skins.

Another control factor is temperature, because fermentation generates heat. Red wines are fermented at higher temperatures to facilitate the extraction of flavor and color, with the generally accepted range being 70 to 90 degrees Fahrenheit. If the temperature climbs too high, the fermentation can boil out of control, creating "cooked" fruit flavors, or it might "stick," which is when the yeast effectively stops working. For white wine, fermentation temperatures are kept between 45 and 60 degrees to preserve "volatile" (i.e., aromatic) compounds and fresher fruit flavors. In cooler regions and/or cellars, it may not be necessary to use any refrigeration for temperature control, but thermo-regulated fermentation vessels have been available for generations.

Inside the fermentation tank where the grape skins rise to the top and create a "cap."

Exceptionally cool fermentations will take longer (some take months), but regardless of the time involved, the process is finished when: (a) the yeasts have run out of sugar to consume, or (b) the winemaker has decided to stop the process early to preserve some residual sugar in the wine. Even "dry" wines may contain up to 10 grams/liter of residual sugar: Because the rising alcohol begins to kill off the yeast, not every bit of sugar in the juice is converted.

Racking, Pressing, Aging

In winemaking, transferring liquid from one vessel to another is called racking. Most white wines are "racked" before fermentation: The pressed juice goes into a tank and sits for a while to let all the solid matter settle at the bottom, after which the clean(er) juice is transferred to a different tank for fermentation.

When a white is finished fermenting, it is transferred either to a clean tank, where it may rest for a bit before an early bottling, or to barrels, where it may age for a year or (much) more. Some wines are aged in mixtures of different vessels: wood barrels of various sizes, egg-shaped concrete vats, stainless steel tanks.

When a red wine is transferred from its fermentation vessel to whatever its aging vessel is destined to be, the process includes pressing all the remaining solids to extract every drop of wine possible. Usually this press wine is added to the free-run juice and the combined mass is put into barrels/tanks for aging. Press wine tends to be a little harsher from the further crushing of skins, seeds, and (sometimes) stems, so sometimes only free-run juice is used. The winemaker may add sulfur dioxide (SO$_2$) to the wine at this point in the process to prevent microbial activity and oxidation during aging. Sulfur is a huge topic of discussion in the wine world these days (see "Sulfites in Wine" on page 17).

Whether it's white or red wine, aging in wood barrels allows for the incremental creep of oxygen via the tiny spaces between the staves of the barrels. This adds complexity and texture to the wine, as well as notes of toast and vanilla leached from the sugars in the wood. Wood also contains tannin, which, for white wines that were fermented without being macerated on their skins, lends an important structural component for aging. Wines aged in concrete or stainless steel are designed to preserve more of their fresh-forward fruit aromas and flavors without any effects of oxidation.

Regardless of the aging vessel, most red wines and some white wines undergo malolactic fermentation, a secondary fermentation initiated by bacteria, not yeast, which facilitates the conversion of sharper malic acid into softer, milkier lactic acid. In white wines especially, the effects of malo are readily discernible in the form of creamy textures and flavors.

While aging, barrels of wine may be racked into different barrels several times along the way, each instance introducing trace amounts of oxygen to the mix, which delicately alters the chemical composition of the wine and affects aroma, color, flavor, and texture. Winemakers may also open a barrel to perform *bâtonnage*, wherein any solids that have collected on the bottom of the barrel (spent yeast cells and other solids, collectively referred to as lees) are stirred up and reintroduced into solution, lending a yeasty quality to the aroma and texture of white wines.

Bottling

After some months, or years, it's time to bottle the wine for sale. There are instances when it will be hand-siphoned right from a barrel into a bottle, but in most cases, the wine is emptied from aging vessels into a neutral tank and subject to a variety of clarification/stabilization treatments before it is bottled and corked. Sometimes, it's as simple as doing one last careful racking before bottling, but usually it's some combination of cold stabilizing, fining, and filtering, followed by a final addition of sulfur.

Cold stabilization, typically used for whites, is when the wine is chilled to a low temperature so that tartaric acid crystals form and precipitate out. Consumers have come to prefer clear, star-bright wines, so treatments like this help wines from appearing hazy or developing (harmless) tartrate crystals in the bottle.

Fining and filtration are also used to clarify and stabilize a wine by removing trace elements that could contribute "off" aromas or flavors. Fining is when the winemaker introduces an agent into the wine that binds with proteins and other suspended particles in the wine to facilitate their precipitating out as sediment. Filtration is what it sounds like: passing the juice through a filter to achieve the same end. Some winemakers argue that fining and filtration remove desirable flavor and aroma compounds along with the undesirable ones.

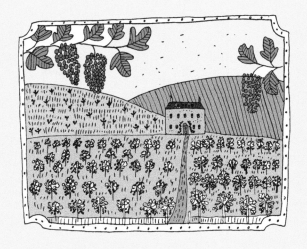

The Life Cycle of a Vineyard

Once a vineyard is planted,
it takes three years before
it produces grapes suitable for wine.
Wine grapes are harvested in
the fall, but a vineyard requires
year-round attention. Here's what's
happening out there.

Winter Pruning

During the cold winter months, vines are in "dormancy" and have no foliage, so winemakers prune to prepare the vine for new growth in the spring. Some growers may also plow, fertilize, or otherwise work their soils during this time.

Bud Break & Flowering

In the early spring (usually March to April in the Northern Hemisphere, and September to October in the Southern Hemisphere), little green buds appear on the vines. They blossom into bright green grape leaves and shoots, then into tiny bunches of flowers, which will eventually turn into grape bunches, provided they're not damaged by wind, frost, or hail.

Fruit Set

Later in the spring, the pollinated flowers lose their petals and become tiny, nascent grapes. At this point, frost, hail, and other natural disasters are still a threat to reduce the overall crop if they damage the developing bunches.

Canopy Management

In addition to converting sunlight into energy, the leaves of a vine provide a shade canopy for the developing grapes. Growers pull and trim leaves constantly during the growing season to modulate the exposure of the grape bunches to the sun—there can't be too much exposure or too little—and to allow air circulation. The grower must also consider the balance of leaves to fruit to make sure the plant is devoting enough of its energy to ripening fruit.

Vineyard Treatments

There are all sorts of pests to manage, which, to the chagrin of many, may include using chemical pesticides. To prevent fungal disease, growers have traditionally sprayed a lique-fied mixture of copper sulfate and lime called "Bordeaux Mixture," which covers leaves and bunches in a silvery-blue dust. Mowing, plowing, or—more controversially—spraying

WINE 101 | 15

chemical herbicides counters weed growth. In spring and summer, growers may also irrigate their vines, though only in those places (mostly the New World—see chapter 6) where it's allowed.

Green Harvesting
Considered an unthinkable sin by those who value quantity above all, "green harvesting" is the practice of removing and discarding grape bunches while they are still green. This is a deliberate thinning of the crop, with the aim of developing greater concentration in those grape bunches that remain on the vine.

Veraison
From July to August (January to February in the Southern Hemisphere) the developing grapes change color from green to "black" (red grapes) or green to yellow-gold (white). The French word *véraison*, like a lot of French wine words, has been adopted by the wider wine world to describe this phenomenon. This is the point where the berries begin to ripen, rather than just grow.

Harvest
It's been an epic journey, and now it's time to pick. The winemaker has measured the levels of acid (tartaric and malic are the main types) and sugar (glucose, fructose) in the grapes. There are countless phenolic compounds, minerals, pectins, and other flavor components that have developed in the grapes over the months. Once the grower makes the call to harvest, it's all hands on deck.

SULFITES IN WINE

Sulfur has been used as an antioxidant/antibacterial in wine since ancient times. In its elemental form, it's a lemon-yellow crystalline substance found near hot springs and volcanoes. In winemaking, it is part of two principal compound chemicals: copper sulfate, a mixture of copper, sulfur, and lime; and sulfur dioxide (SO_2), a gas with a pungent struck-match smell. Copper sulfate is diluted with water and sprayed on vines/grapes as a fungicide (even organic vineyards permit its use); SO_2, meanwhile, is not typically added to wine as a gas but rather converted to a powder.

SO_2 may be used at a variety of points in the winemaking process, including: harvest/crush, where it is sometimes used on the just-picked fruit to inhibit wild yeast activity and prevent the oxidation of any ruptured grapes; fermentation, where it will kill unwanted yeasts and bacteria; and bottling, again as a disinfectant/preservative.

Although there are many other additives used in winemaking, sulfites are the most talked about. They can be toxic to those who have to spray or work with them, they can cause allergic reactions (especially in people with asthma), they can lend unpleasant (rotten egg, burned match) smells to wines at higher concentrations, and they're anathema to those who feel nothing whatsoever should be added to a wine other than grapes and yeast. Natural winemakers try to eliminate sulfite use altogether or use only minimal amounts at bottling. This practice requires extra-careful fruit handling, extremely sanitary winery conditions, and a little bit of luck.

In addition to laws requiring producers to notify consumers if a wine contains sulfites, there are limits placed on the total quantity of sulfites allowed in wine, measured in "parts per million." Interestingly, wine is one of the few products required to say "Contains Sulfites" on its label.

VARIETAL WINES & BLENDS

When we think of the word "blend" as it relates to wine, we think of two (or more) grape varieties combined to create a wine that is greater than the sum of its parts. Bordeaux, in France, may be the most famous example of a region known for blended wines. The reds combine Cabernet Sauvignon, Merlot, Cabernet Franc, and others in myriad ways. In Old World Europe especially, the place name of a wine takes precedence over the grape name, to the point where grape varieties may not be mentioned on the label at all.

In the United States (and other parts of the New World), wines are labeled with the name of the grape featured prominently. Most of these "varietal" wines are not composed entirely of the stated variety, however. Laws differ around the world, but most varietal wines are required to contain only 75 percent to 85 percent of the grape named on the label. They will obviously taste strongly of the dominant grape, but technically, they're blends, too.

As different grapes ripen at different times, most winemakers harvest and vinify them separately, then blend the finished wines in their desired proportions before aging. But there are also blends that comprise wines from the same grape grown in different vineyard sites. Then there are field blends, which are blends of grapes in the vineyard itself. A wine described as a field blend is often a wine that contains multiple grapes that are co-planted in a vineyard and harvested and fermented together.

There is no hotter topic right now than natural wine. People have written entire books on it, and there are surely more to come, as producers and consumers alike have embraced a style of winemaking that aims to eliminate inputs—particularly chemical ones—at every step of the winemaking process. It's a noble goal, but one that is difficult to achieve at scale. It has also sparked a lot of debate among wine experts over the quality and style of these wines. In creating natural wine, growers must:

► Grow grapes organically and hand harvest with no chemical pesticides, fertilizers, or herbicides (copper sulfate sprays are typically allowed)

► Not use cultured/commercial yeasts or added sugar

► Not make adjustments to the acid levels in the wine, or "water back" a wine to bring its alcohol level down

► Not add enzymes (proteins)

► Make every effort to eliminate sulfites completely (except for those naturally produced in the grapes), although many producers will add a small amount at bottling

► Not augment wines with additives like concentrated grape must, color enhancers, and oak chips; when oak barrels are used for aging, they are most often reclaimed barrels, as new ones are thought to impart too strong a character to the wine

► Not apply treatments such as "micro-oxygenation" (an injection of oxygen into the must, which softens tannins) or "reverse osmosis" (a filtration that reduces alcohol)

► Keep fining and filtering to a bare minimum or avoid them all together.

Organic and biodynamic viticulture/winemaking practices apply all of these criteria and essentially "put numbers" to or quantify the practices. Biodynamics is a slightly more holistic, even spiritual approach to agriculture influenced by the teachings of Austrian philosopher Rudolf Steiner (1861–1925). There are assorted third-party organizations or agencies around the world that outline the standards to qualify for organic and biodynamic certification, including our own USDA National Organic Program (NOP).

WHAT'S IN A BOTTLE?

Between the organic compounds derived from the seeds, skins, and juice of grapes—sugars, acids, phenolic compounds (tannins)—and the hundreds of compounds produced by the biochemical reactions of fermentation, wine is an extremely complex beverage. And yet it is still mostly water. Note the average concentrations of the major chemical components of wine:

- Water: **82 percent**
- Ethanol: **12 percent**
- Vitamins and Minerals: **2 percent**
- Acids: **1.5 percent**
- Glycerol and Other Sugars: **1 percent**
- Tannins and Phenolics (Flavonoids, Resveratrol, Anthocyanins, etc.): **1 percent**
- Sulfites: **0.5 percent**

A typical bottle contains 750ml, or 25.4 ounces, of wine. In addition to the trace sugars in the wine (especially sweeter wines), alcohol itself contains calories. In fact, while a gram of sugar has four calories, alcohol has seven. The average calorie content in a full bottle of wine is 600, meaning a typical five-ounce glass contains around 120 calories. These figures vary widely based on alcohol content and residual sugar content in the wine.

WHAT'S ON A BOTTLE?

The "Old World" winemaking countries of Europe—France, Italy, Spain, Germany, Portugal, etc.—prioritize the name of the place a wine is made above all else. Driven by the concept of "terroir," which centers on the natural environment that shapes a wine, "appellations" are geographically delimited territories (AOC, DOC, DO) that are classified as official "denominations of origin." These place names were really the first "brands" in the world of wine, and they're still important—often printed in much bigger letters than the name of the producer!

Type of wine

Region where wine is made

Grand Cru is the highest level of vineyard desig- nation in France

CORTON-CHARLEMAGNE

Grand Cru

APPELLATION CORTON CHARRLEMAGNE CONTROLEE

WHITE BURGUNDY WINE

— • —

ALC 13.5% BYVOL   **J-F. COCHE-DURY**   750 ML

PROPRIETAIRE VITICULTEUR A MEURSAULT (COTE D'OR)

PRODUCT OF FRANCE

Alcohol by volume

Village where winery is located

Name of the producer

Size of bottle

In *"New World"* winemaking countries like the United States, Australia, New Zealand, Chile, and Argentina, wines are typically labeled with more emphasis on the grape variety and the producer, although place names are also still an important part of the mix.

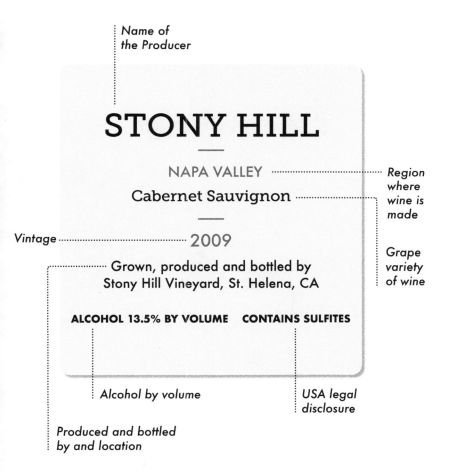

Name of the Producer

STONY HILL

NAPA VALLEY

Cabernet Sauvignon

2009

Grown, produced and bottled by
Stony Hill Vineyard, St. Helena, CA

ALCOHOL 13.5% BY VOLUME   CONTAINS SULFITES

Region where wine is made

Grape variety of wine

Vintage

Alcohol by volume

USA legal disclosure

Produced and bottled by and location

Fortified Wines: Sweet or Dry?

Fortified wines are produced in sweet and dry styles. The difference is based on when the fortification actually takes place. In the early stages of fermentation, there is sugar left that the yeast still needs to convert to alcohol. Adding a distilled grape spirit earlier in the process will halt the fermentation, leaving residual sugar and thus a sweeter style of wine. This is more common in Port production.

Small, temperature-controlled stainless steel fermentation tanks.

2

WINE BUILDS CHARACTER

The overarching goal in learning about wine? To decipher the characteristics that you most enjoy. Here's how. When you take a sip, a wine's chemical structure reacts with your sense receptors. At that moment, you will perceive a wine's different flavor compounds. Once you are familiar with the characteristics of wine described in this chapter, you will understand how wine chemistry affects your own perception.

BODY

When we describe the body of a wine, we can classify it into one of three main categories: light, medium, and full. Although these terms are not scientific, they do allow the taster to place the wine on what I call a texture spectrum. The easiest way to understand body in wine is to think of it as weight. If we use milk as an example, at one end of the spectrum we have skim milk, watery and extremely light; then there's 2-percent milk, with slightly more weight than skim; then whole milk, which is far weightier. Wine is exactly the same. On one end of the spectrum you have light, crisp white wine, such as Italian Pinot Bianco; then medium-weight like California Chardonnay; and, finally, full-bodied whites with richness in mouthfeel like Sauternes, a sweet wine from Bordeaux. Of course, much like everything with wine, body becomes more complex with other contributors like alcohol, residual sugar, and oak aging.

TANNIN

Tannin plays an incredibly interesting role in wine, mostly with reds. Tannin is felt as dryness on the palate or tartness sensed by the tongue. Tannin helps a wine age for extended lengths of time. There are two principal tannins that occur naturally in the winemaking process: fruit tannin, from the skins of the grape; and wood tannin, from the seeds, stems, and barrels. These phenolic compounds are more concentrated in certain grape varieties like Cabernet Sauvignon and other thick-skinned red grapes, and they can be intensified during the winemaking process. One example is when whole grape clusters are included in the fermentation of red wine, meaning the stems are included in the juice. In winemaking, you allow grape juice to soak with the skins and stems (called maceration) to extract the tannins that shape the mouthfeel of the resulting wine. Maceration resembles what we do when we steep tea in hot water. If you want to feel powerful tannins in a wine, look no further than the "black" wines of Cahors, in southwestern France, which are made from the inky Malbec grape and often see extended aging in wood.

Tannins are antioxidants, meaning they bind with oxygen molecules and prevent wine from oxidizing prematurely. Studies have shown that the antioxidant properties of tannins help with human aging as well; compounds like resveratrol contribute high-density lipoproteins and protect against cholesterol buildup.

ACIDITY

I've been called an "acid hound," which is to say an oenophile who searches out mouthwatering, zippy, crisp white wines. It's true, I gravitate to whites with high acidity. So how does wine end up this way? There are a dozen or more types of acids that show up in a finished wine, but we'll focus on three naturally occurring organic acids—tartaric, citric, and malic. These acids are responsible for protecting the stability of the wine and for the sour, lip-smacking freshness you experience when tasting. To experience a high-acid white wine, try a New Zealand Sauvignon Blanc produced on the South Island. Because this is a cool-climate region, grapes are able to mature more slowly and retain their naturally high acids.

Tartaric acid is the grape's natural preservative. It's important in wine for color preservation and also for enhancing the effectiveness of SO_2 for overall wine preservation. Through the cycle of grape-growing and winemaking, this acid can become highly concentrated. Often the winemaker will opt to cold stabilize, a process whereby the finished wine is chilled to 40 degrees Fahrenheit for two weeks and tartaric acid molecules bind together, forming glass-like crystals, which are filtered out. Sometimes these crystals will appear in a bottle of wine or on the underside of a cork, which is perfectly harmless.

Citric acid is naturally occurring at relatively weak levels in wine grapes (much higher in fruits like lemons and limes), which is why it is important to understand how to preserve the small amounts that do exist. Picking the grapes when "green," just before ripeness, captures the most citric acidity. In production areas like Champagne, where they harvest comparatively early, wines boast sharper, brighter acidity profiles.

Malic acid is found in nearly every fruit and is prominent in green apples, so it's often referred to as "green apple" acidity. The malic acid level in a wine may be high enough that the winemaker opts to perform a process called malolactic conversion, which changes the harder malic acid into the softer lactic acids associated with dairy. This conversion has a by-product called diacetyl, which smells like butter. This is how a winemaker produces a "buttery" Chardonnay. Malic acid is also important for vine health as it assists in energy conversion during the gestation cycle of producing fruit year in and year out.

SWEETNESS

All wine starts as sweet grape must that is then fermented to convert sugar to alcohol. Yeast is the catalyst for this conversion. Most fermentations are imperfect, meaning a finished wine is almost always left with some unfermented sugar, called "residual sugar" (RS). One of the most enjoyable and affordable examples of a wine with residual sugar is Moscato d'Asti from Piedmont, Italy.

Another way a winemaker can achieve a sweet wine is either by arresting the fermentation with the addition of a distilled spirit, which immobilizes the yeasts, or by adding sugar after fermentation. Champagne is a great example where growers add sugar after fermentation, to adjust sweetness levels, with a process called the liqueur d'expédition.

ALCOHOL

Nearly anything that contains sugar can be fermented into alcohol with the addition of yeast. The specific type of alcohol from fermented fruit sugars is ethanol C_2H_6O, safe and enjoyable to consume with some care. There is a broad spectrum of the amount of alcohol found in wine and in the United States, a federal labeling regulation requires you to place the alcohol strength, known as alcohol by volume (abv), in print on each label. This is the best way to understand the power or strength of what you are consuming. Today there is a trend for lower alcohol wine; German Riesling is often produced "off-dry" with a small amount of residual sugar and abvs of 9 to 11 percent. Heftier red wines, like Port from the Douro region of Portugal, have typical abvs between 20 and 22 percent. A normal range for still red and white wine is 11- to 14.5-percent abv.

Wine's Balancing Act

When wine is "in balance," it's much harder to pick out singular components: The fruit, acid, and tannin are working together. To recognize more clearly the major elements in a wine, try these exercises:

Body	Sip water, clear juice, then milk, not for flavor but for texture. Take a big sip and roll the liquid around in your mouth.
Citric Acid	Squeeze lemon juice in your mouth and wait to recognize the salivary reaction.
Tannin	Oversteep a black or green tea, then taste, acknowledging the dryness left after you expectorate or swallow.
Fruit Tannin	Peel the skin off a plum and chew only the skin, identifying the tight, tart astringency left in the mouth.

Dining alfresco at Tenuta Sette Cieli on the Tuscan coast.

3

STYLE AND SUBSTANCE

Developing your taste memory is the best way to start recognizing your likes and dislikes when it comes to wine. Make notes. Take photos. But most important, be open to new experiences. Professional sommeliers often join tasting groups to share the costs of doing side-by-side comparisons. The home version of this is to invite a few friends over and pull some corks. As a guide for you when choosing or purchasing wine, here's a breakdown of the major wine styles, ordered from lightest to boldest, and representative examples (with rough cost estimates: $ = $20 or less; $$ = $20 to $30; $$$ = $30 or more) from around the world.

SPARKLING WINES

Effervescence in wine comes from carbon dioxide gas produced during fermentation. Bubbles float to the surface and dissipate, creating a frothy "mousse." The intensity of effervescence varies, as do fruit flavors and sweetness levels, depending on the chosen grape varieties, climate and soil, and method of production.

Although some cheap sparklers are simply force-carbonated, most quality sparkling wine is produced in one of three ways: the Traditional, or Champagne Method; the Tank, or Charmat Method; or the Ancestral Method.

The traditional method, or Méthode Champenoise, is the most time-consuming and labor-intensive, though it is also believed to produce the best wines. It starts with finished still wine that is bottled, supplemented with a sugar/yeast mixture called liqueur de tirage, then sealed; a second fermentation ensues and CO_2 builds up in the bottle. Over time, spent yeasts precipitate into a whitish sediment, which is expelled from the bottle in a process called disgorgement (often done by hand). Afterward, a small amount of sugar, called a dosage (doh-SAHJ), is usually added to "correct" the sweetness and texture of these high-acid wines.

When tasting Champagne Method wines, residual sugar (RS) will affect your perception, as it does in all wines. Champagne has official sweetness classifications based on grams of sugar per liter, although what you're really evaluating in most cases is a wine's degree of dryness:

- ▶ Brut Nature: 0 to 3 grams/liter
- ▶ Extra Brut: 0 to 6 g/l
- ▶ Brut: 0 to 12 g/l
- ▶ Extra-Dry: 12 to 17 g/l
- ▶ Dry: 17 to 32 g/l
- ▶ Demi-Sec: 32 to 50 g/l
- ▶ Doux: 50+ g/l

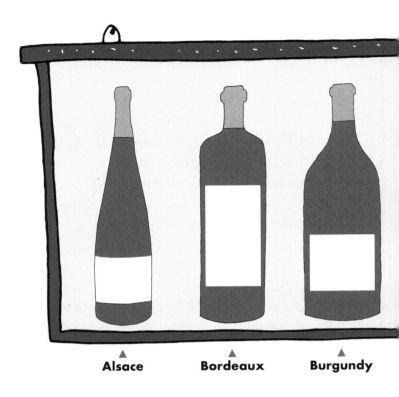

| Alsace | Bordeaux | Burgundy |

Demi-Sec and Doux are the only truly sweet wines in the bunch. Additionally, because Champagne Method wines are left in contact with their lees (spent yeasts) for extended periods, you'll detect yeast-derived notes of bread dough, toast, and chopped nuts.

The Tank or Charmat Method mimics the Champagne Method, but on a larger scale and with fewer steps. Wine and the sugar/yeast solution are combined in large, pressurized tanks. When the second fermentation is complete, the wine is kept under pressure while it is filtered, given a *dosage*, then bottled.

Ancestral Method sparklers are wines that are bottled and capped/corked before they've completed fermentation, trapping whatever CO_2 is produced as it finishes up. These

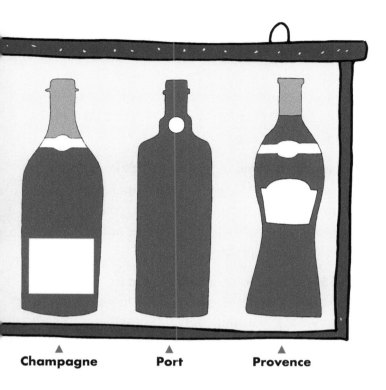

| Champagne | Port | Provence |

wines often contain yeast sediment, and their carbonation is usually more delicate.

The following are the major sparkling wine styles. Many experts insist that these wines be served ice-cold, which reduces pressure in the bottle and keeps foaming to a minimum, but you will discover greater nuance if you let them rise to about 50 degrees.

Champagne ($$$) Champagne is the gold standard. Hailing from one of Europe's coolest regions, and rarely exceeding 12.5 percent alcohol, Champagne nevertheless feels substantial. Crafted from combinations of Chardonnay, Pinot Noir, and Pinot Meunier grown in chalky limestone, these wines taste of minerals, tart apples, lemon zest, nuts, and bread dough.

California Sparklers ($$–$$$) California sparklers are a diverse and high-quality lot, most of them modeled closely on Champagne, and in some cases crafted by Californian outposts of famous French Champagne houses, such as Roederer, Taittinger, and Moët & Chandon.

Cava ($–$$) Cava is produced mostly in Spain's Penedès region, from Macabeo, Parellada, and Xarello grapes. It is a well-priced Champagne Method wine. Cava is typically more floral and a touch lighter than Champagne, but still tantalizingly close in overall quality.

Franciacorta ($$) Franciacorta is an appellation in Lombardy, Italy, where producers focus on the "Champagne" grapes (Chardonnay and Pinot Noir) and Méthode Champenoise to produce wines that often compare favorably to French versions.

Crémant ($–$$) Crémant is a term for French sparklers made using the Champagne Method but in regions outside of Champagne (Burgundy, Alsace, Jura, etc.). They offer lower-cost alternatives to Champagne and are often made from the same grapes.

Sekt ($–$$) Sekt is German sparkling wine made in either the Tank or Champagne Method, often from the Riesling grape, which tends to create more ethereal, aromatic sparkling wine.

Pétillant-Naturel ($–$$) Pétillant-Naturel describes fizzy wines made in the Ancestral Method. There are excellent examples in France's Loire Valley, especially Vouvray, where they craft tart, apple/pear-fruited, yeasty styles from Chenin Blanc.

Prosecco ($) Prosecco is an Italian specialty based on the Glera grape. It's perhaps the best-known Tank Method sparkler, with peach/apricot fruit and a softer, sweeter feel relative to Champagne.

LIGHT-BODIED WHITE WINE

One of the main determinants of body is alcohol by volume, because one by-product of fermentation is glycerol, an alcohol sugar that lends viscosity. In general, light-bodied whites fall below 12.5 percent abv and are aged less than a year. Another factor in body is whether the wine was aged in wood barrels, which may impart wood sugars and tannins.

Assessing body involves measuring the wine's weight on your palate. Your perception of what's "light" or "full" may differ from that of others (much like perceptions of sweetness vary). Most of the wines listed here, however, will spark no debate; they are marked by fresh, tart flavors and textures, and little to no oak influence. Whites are best served chilled, between 50 and 55 degrees Fahrenheit.

Loire Valley Sauvignon Blanc ($$–$$$) Loire Valley Sauvignon Blanc has a stony, flinty, citrusy quality and is grown in regions such as Sancerre and Pouilly-Fumé.

Muscadet ($–$$) Muscadet is grown near the mouth of the Loire River, on France's north Atlantic coast. It is a deeply mineral, saline white from the Melon de Bourgogne grape.

Grüner Veltliner ($–$$) Grüner Veltliner is a specialty of Austria's Danube River Valley appellations, such as Wachau. Grüner means "green" and there are indeed green fruit and herb notes, along with citrusy acidity and crystalline minerality. Austrian Riesling is another tart and refreshing light-bodied choice.

Gavi ($–$$) Gavi is a region in Piedmont, Italy, where wines often resemble the mineral-etched whites of Chablis. The local Cortese grape grows in chalky soils and tastes of citrus, white flowers, and stones.

Vinho Verde ($) Vinho Verde (translated as "green" or young wine) is so named because it is released very young, usually within six months of the harvest. This northern Portuguese specialty is a tart, citrusy, sometimes spritzy white from native varieties, including Alvarinho and Loureiro.

MEDIUM-BODIED WHITE WINE

Measured in abv, medium-bodied whites fall in the 12.5 percent to 14 percent range and are more likely to have aged in wood barrels. Outside of those characteristics, you'll encounter many variations among these wines.

Chablis ($$–$$$) Chablis is from northern Burgundy, France, and is one of the world's iconic Chardonnays. It is full of minerality and lemony acidity, with notes of green and yellow apple, and little to no oak.

Loire Valley Chenin Blanc ($–$$$) Loire Valley Chenin Blanc, from appellations such as Vouvray, Montlouis, and Saumur, is high in acid yet with a texture and a quince/apple fruit component that lands it in the medium-bodied range.

California Sauvignon Blanc ($–$$$) California Sauvignon Blanc is an amorphous category, with some wines displaying more of the citrus zing of the Loire

Valley but others taking on tropical notes and the creamy richness of white Bordeaux.

Friulano ($–$$$) Friulano is a Sauvignon Blanc cousin from northeast Italy. It features stony minerality, white flowers, and peach/apricot notes. It's usually unoaked.

Oregon Pinot Gris ($–$$) Oregon Pinot Gris often resembles Chardonnay, albeit with a more floral component to its aromas. It is lower in acid than grapes like Sauvignon Blanc and Riesling, with pear and melon fruit notes.

FULL-BODIED WHITE WINE

Usually north of 14 percent alcohol and aged in oak, fuller-bodied whites are not the sole province of warmer climates, but it stands to reason that more sun and more heat result in "more" wine.

Châteauneuf-du-Pape Blanc ($$$) Châteauneuf-du-Pape Blanc is a blend of grapes native to France's southern Rhône Valley. The principal variety is the richly textured Grenache Blanc, supported by the fleshy Roussanne and higher-acid Clairette and Picpoul. These are palate-coating whites with notes of honeysuckle and yellow peach.

California Chardonnay ($$–$$$) California Chardonnay is best known for yellow apple and lemon/tangerine flavors, medium to low acidity, and a touch of vanilla and buttered toast from oak aging. The range of styles today is quite broad.

Bordeaux Blanc ($–$$$) Bordeaux Blanc is a blend of citrusy Sauvignon Blanc and waxier, creamier Sémillon. Higher-priced styles typically incorporate fermentation/ aging in new French oak barrels, lending notes of brioche toast and vanilla.

Rioja Blanco ($–$$$) Rioja Blanco, like white Bordeaux, is variable; some styles are crisper, while others are aged in oak or in the bottle for extended periods and develop toasty, nutty richness. The main grape is Viura, which has tropical flavors and medium-low acidity.

AROMATIC WHITE WINES

Stepping aside from body, some people enjoy drinking what they smell over what they feel and are attracted to aromatic wines. To this end, I present here some wines made from grapes that are richer in the chemical compounds that lend aroma to wine.

Wines made from aromatic varieties often smell sweet, which is not technically possible but reflects our tendency to associate certain smells with things that taste sweet. Dry whites can play tricks on you: Their exotic aromas give an impression of sweetness even when the wine contains little to no residual sugar.

Condrieu ($$$) Condrieu is a small region in France's Northern Rhône Valley specializing in textured, headily perfumed wines from the Viognier grape. It offers chamomile/herbal aromas as well as notes of beeswax and richer citrus fruits.

Gewürztraminer ($$–$$$) Gewürztraminer is perhaps the most notoriously perfumed grape in the world, with aromas of stone fruit, lychee, rose petals, ginger, and nutmeg. Its most acclaimed expressions are grown in Alsace, France.

German Riesling ($–$$$) German Riesling ranges from very light-bodied and dry/off-dry to rich and unctuous, as you move up the spectrum from wines harvested early to wines harvested later. The variety's high-powered aromas include wildflowers, white peaches, wet stones, and, in richer, more concentrated versions, petrol and brown spices.

Torrontés ($–$$) Torrontés is Argentina's signature white grape, known for assertively floral aromas and lightweight mouthfeel. Usually unoaked, it has notes of ripe peach and apricot, and is of medium acidity.

New Zealand Sauvignon Blanc ($–$$) New Zealand Sauvignon Blanc is the most pungent expression of this variety, with scents of gooseberries, bell pepper, herbs, grapefruit, and more tropical fruits such as guava and mango.

ROSÉ WINES

Rosé is made from red grapes that have been left in contact with their skins just long enough (anywhere from a few hours to a few days) to impart some of their color, tannin, and flavor compounds. There are many shades of rosé, owing not only to the color pigmentation of the grape(s) used but also to the length of maceration. Serve rosé at temperatures similar to white.

Champagne Rosé ($$$) Champagne Rosé is crafted from Pinot Noir and/or Pinot Meunier and is extremely complex, with an aromatic, rich texture and weight, and compelling acid with long finish of flavor. In addition to redcurrant, pink grapefruit, and wild strawberries, you'll find earthier aromas of stones, dried flowers, bread dough, smoke, and toasted nuts.

Provence ($–$$$) Provence is the region in the south of France around Marseille known for its spicy, salmon-pink rosés. Grown along the Mediterranean coast, most famously in Bandol, grapes such as Grenache and Mourvèdre are turned into rosés with floral, mineral notes to complement their tart currant and wild strawberry fruit. Hints of lavender and other herbs lend aromatic intrigue.

Pinot Noir Rosé ($$) Pinot Noir Rosé from Burgundy, California, and Oregon presents a great opportunity to experience a "noble" grape variety in rosé form. Brisk acidity supports notes of cranberry, strawberry, cherry, and other tart red fruits.

Nebbiolo Rosato ($$) Nebbiolo Rosato from the Piedmont and Lombardy regions of Italy is another example of a "noble" grape in rosé form, with spicy, earthy notes to complement the fruit component.

LIGHT-BODIED RED WINES

Light-bodied reds are often categorized as having 12.5 percent alcohol or less. There is a more subtle influence of barrel aging on most of these styles. Thanks to their bright acidity and relatively low alcohol, these wines are especially versatile with food and should be served at cellar temperature, 55 degrees Fahrenheit.

Red Burgundy ($$–$$$) Red Burgundy is considered the quintessential Pinot Noir. Styles can reach into the medium- and full-bodied categories as well. Dark cherry fruit is suffused with notes of underbrush and minerals. Tannins are firmer compared to New World Pinot Noirs.

Jura Reds ($$) Jura Reds, from grapes such as Poulsard and Trousseau, are uniquely delicate. Located in eastern France, Jura is a wild and bucolic region known for reds that taste like fresh-picked wild raspberries and other woodland fruits.

Willamette Valley Pinot Noir ($$) Willamette Valley Pinot Noir has achieved worldwide recognition relatively quickly (the first Pinot Noir was planted in the region in the 1960s). Cherry fruited, delicately smoky/ earthy, and lively, these are softly contoured reds with cool-climate freshness.

Galician Red Wine ($$) Galician Red Wine, from appellations such as Ribeira Sacra in Spain, are usually dominated by the Mencía variety, which has a tangy, dark-fruited profile and even a peppery, herbaceous note. These wines often graduate into the medium-bodied category, showing firm tannins and notes of cranberry, pomegranate, and violets.

Beaujolais ($–$$) Beaujolais is at the southern end of France's Burgundy region and is known for brightly fruited reds from the Gamay grape. Gamay displays kindred qualities to Pinot Noir—soft tannins, crunchy berry fruit—although it tends to be a little juicier.

MEDIUM-BODIED RED WINES

Climbing up the weight scale means encountering a little more tannin (derived from grapes and/or wood barrels) and a little more alcohol (12.5 percent to 14.5 percent).

It does not necessarily mean the wine will have a darker color; some dark-hued reds are in fact quite lightweight, and vice versa. Serve weightier reds at 60 to 65 degrees.

Northern Rhône Syrah ($$–$$$) Northern Rhône Syrah ranges from medium- to full-bodied, depending on the appellation from which it hails. It displays a darker, purplish color and aromas of black/blue fruits (berries, plums), roasted meat, black pepper, lavender, and olive.

Rioja ($$–$$$) Rioja is Spain's most famous red wine region, where the Tempranillo variety shows cherry kirsch flavors and cedary, chocolatey notes from long aging in barrels. These wines are typically very silky, with hints of tobacco on the finish.

California Pinot Noir ($$–$$$) California Pinot Noir is most often a more luscious, fruit-forward expression of Pinot Noir than wines from the Old World (e.g., Burgundy). Aromas and flavors of cherries, wild berries, cola, vanilla, underbrush, and violets characterize these plush-textured wines.

Sangiovese ($$) Sangiovese can be light-bodied, but as expressed in the Tuscan trio of Chianti, Nobile di Montepulciano, and Brunello di Montalcino, it is medium. Known for high acidity and medium tannin, Sangiovese is woodsy and slightly smoky, with hints of spicy black cherry fruit, violets, and earth.

Loire Valley Cabernet Franc ($–$$) Loire Valley Cabernet Franc, as grown in appellations such as Bourgueil and Chinon, has a meatier mid-palate characterized by black plums, cranberries, bell pepper, and wet clay notes.

The Curious Case of "Orange" Wine

Wines made from white grapes that are left to macerate on their skins during fermentation are no longer oddities. So-called "orange" wines are an ever-growing category and present a range of hues for the taster to consider. Some whites crafted this way may have a rosé-like hue, especially wines made from Pinot Gris/Grigio, whose "gray" skins, if left in contact with the juice even briefly, will lend the wine a pink or copper cast, like northeast Italy's *ramato*-style Pinot Grigio.

The longer-macerated styles, some of which are fermented in open-topped containers or wood barrels and are therefore more exposed to oxygen, can be as orange or caramel colored as certain styles of Sherry or Madeira. If the wine in question is meant to be a dry, still, unfortified white, look for vibrancy of color—bright rather than "browned" orange—in making your quality assessment.

FULL-BODIED RED WINES

We are regularly seeing wines with abvs in the 15 percent to 16 percent range and higher, which isn't a problem if the wine has enough acidity to keep everything in balance. Anything above 14 percent is considered full-bodied. Fuller-bodied reds often originate in warmer climates and develop richness from aging in oak barrels.

Barolo ($$$) Barolo is from Piedmont, Italy, and is made from the Nebbiolo grape, which has a deceptively light hue. The wines are nevertheless high in alcohol and tannin and are headily aromatic, with scents of dried red and black cherries, redcurrant, tobacco, tar, rose petals, balsamic, wet leaves, and leather.

Brunello di Montalcino ($$$) Brunello di Montalcino is Tuscany's most powerful expression of the Sangiovese grape. Woodsy black-cherry fruit is supported with notes of cedar and chocolate from long aging in oak barrels.

Amarone ($$$) Amarone is a specialty of northern Italy's Valpolicella region and is made from grapes that are dried after harvest to concentrate their sugars. It has a rich, syrupy red and black fruit character with notes of toffee, leather, and warm spice.

Zinfandel ($$–$$$) Considered America's heritage grape, Zinfandel often comes from very old vines. Black plums, brandied cherries, coffee, chocolate, and dusty earth are all common traits in these wines, which tend to be high in alcohol but low in acidity and tannin.

Bordeaux/Napa Valley Cabernet Sauvignon ($$–$$$) Cabernet from Bordeaux and Napa is rich, structured, and dense, characterized by cassis, black raspberry, plum, cigar box, cedar, and hints of herbs and bay leaf. Hard tannins provide structural underpinning.

Washington State Reds ($$–$$$) Washington reds are produced mostly in the arid eastern half of the state and include plummy, voluptuous Bordeaux-style blends and noteworthy wines from Syrah.

Châteauneuf-du-Pape ($$–$$$) Châteauneuf-du-Pape is the signature red wine of France's southern Rhône Valley, produced from a wide-ranging blend of grapes but typically driven by Grenache Noir grown in sandy, pebbly soils. Aromas of wild herbs, lavender, and licorice accent a rich core of jammy fruit and support a rich, viscous texture.

Australian Shiraz ($–$$$) Australian Shiraz is an inky and explosive expression of the Syrah grape. The color is often nearly black, the texture luscious, and the flavors a tangle of mulberries, blackcurrants, warm spices, black pepper, licorice, and often a hint of eucalyptus.

Argentine Malbec ($–$$$) Argentine Malbec is dense, purple-fruited, and tannic. Black cherry, blackberry, pomegranate, dark chocolate, and violets dominate.

DESSERT WINES

Dessert wine is sweet. Most become sweet through diverse means of extracting water from the juice, thereby concentrating grape sugars. Alternately, a famous dessert wine, Vintage Port, is fortified with grape brandy before fermentation has a chance to finish. Depending on the style of sweet wine, they are either: (a) fortified wines with unfermented sugars, or (b) they contain more sugar than is possible to convert to alcohol.

Eiswein ($$$) Eiswein is German, usually from Riesling, and harvested so late the grapes actually freeze, dehydrating and concentrating them. These are rich, fruit-driven wines, with juicy yellow peach fruit supported by fresh acidity.

Sauternes and Barsac ($$–$$$) Sauternes and Barsac are two of the sweet wine regions of Bordeaux, where Sauvignon Blanc and Sémillon grapes wither on the vine well into the fall. A gray mold called Botrytis grows on the grapes, dehydrates them, and concentrates their sugars. The result? Sweet, golden nectars with flavors of wildflower honey, grilled peaches, honeycomb, apricots, hazelnuts, and citrus.

Vin Santo ($$–$$$) Vin Santo is a nectar produced in Italy, especially Tuscany, from white grapes that are dried into raisins, pressed, fermented, and aged in very small barrels. These wines are amber-colored and are nuttier and more caramelized than Sauternes.

Port ($$–$$$) Port is Portugal's historic fortified wine from the Douro Valley. There are several styles of Port, the best-known being the densely fruited, sweet Vintage Port, which is bottled right after it has been fortified and is capable of aging for many decades.

Moscato d'Asti ($) Moscato d'Asti is a lightweight, semi-sparkling (*frizzante*) Italian white made from Moscato grapes. Winemakers arrest the fermentation before it has finished. It contains notes of peach and white flowers.

BARCELONA X
MADRID X

ANDALUCÍA
Jerez

Sherry

Sherry is a labor-intensive fortified wine produced in the region of Jerez at the southern tip of Spain. These food-friendly, high-acid wines are based primarily on the Palomino grape and are fortified at different times depending on style. Those styles are:

Manzanilla	crisp, nutty, salty
Fino	pale color, light, tangy
Amontillado	darker, hazelnuts, dried fruit (dry or slightly sweet)
Oloroso	amber color, dry, long aged, oxidative, dense
Pedro Ximénez	dark, sweet style from sun-dried Ximénez grapes

4

HOW TO
TASTE WINE

Tasting like a sommelier is a step-by-step process that fully engages your senses. It seems geeky and excessive until you try it and realize how much it enhances and contextualizes what's in your glass. It entails more than merely taking a sip and swishing the wine around like mouthwash. Aspiring sommeliers and casual tasters alike should become well-versed in "the grid," which covers the four basic steps of wine tasting: sight, smell, taste, and evaluation. The grid is your road map to tasting like a pro.

Here's Looking at You

Looking at a wine can tell you a lot. Color, clarity, intensity, and visual viscosity tell you about the grape, climate, age, body, whether or not it was aged in oak, whether it was filtered, and what flaws it may have. Yes—with practice, you can deduce all of that through appearance alone.

Ever see a sommelier hold a glass up to the light and gaze at it pensively, as if anointing a new Lion King? This is one way to assess clarity, but the best way to judge a wine's appearance is to view it against a white backdrop—a tablecloth or sheet of paper—in a well-lit area. Pour a small amount of wine into a glass, two to three ounces, enough to swirl and sip, and tilt the glass away from you. Look at that oval of liquid and you'll see it is darker in the center, or "core," then becomes lighter at the edge, or "rim." Here's what to look for and what it will tell you:

COLOR

White wines range from "water clear" to deep burnished gold, depending on their age, grape variety, use of oak (or not), and other factors. Thanks to gradual oxidation, white wines gain deeper color as they age. Too much "browning," however, and the wine is either past its prime or faulty. Conversely, many young white wines have flecks of green among the yellows and golds.

White grapes contain less pigmentation than reds, but there is a white-wine color spectrum: Riesling and Sauvignon Blanc, for example, skew straw-yellow/silver/green. Chardonnay is typically a deeper yellow-gold. Oak-aged whites, meanwhile, have a deeper cast, as they literally breathe small amounts of oxygen through the tiny cracks between the barrel staves.

In contrast, red wines lose color as they age, moving from a deep, vibrant garnet/ruby/purple in their youth to a lighter brick red/orange/amber. This, too, is the effect of oxidation, which in red wines includes tannin molecules binding together over time and precipitating out of solution as sediment. There are lots of dissolved solids in red wines, leading to instances when a young red wine is nearly or fully opaque, a sign of a very full-bodied, and possibly unfiltered, style.

Red grapes also vary in hue. This is often attributed to the relative thickness of their skins, but actually, color in red wine owes to a variety of factors. Pinot Noir is usually more lightly colored (a cherry red), while Syrah is much darker, inky-purple, nearly black at times. Another factor influencing red wine color is acidity. The chemistry of red wine is such that wines with higher acid are more discernably red in color while those with lower acidity tend toward purple/blue.

INTENSITY

Whites and reds alike tend to be brighter and more saturated in color—even if it's a lighter color—when they're young. Certain wines will display the same color all the way from the core to the rim, an indicator of both youth and, usually, a fuller-bodied style.

In all cases, like photos on a windowsill that have been bleached by the sun, red and white wines alike become less vivid or intensely colored over time. How long they're able to retain their youthful hue is a good indicator of the quality of both the wine and its storage conditions.

VISCOSITY

Swirl the wine in your glass. Does it cling to the sides, forming "legs" or "tears"? This is an indicator of viscosity, which denotes the presence of glycerol and alcohol in the wine. The more viscous the liquid, the more full-bodied and higher in alcohol the wine.

STEP TWO

The Nose Knows

It makes sense that what we smell affects what we taste. So smelling, or "nosing," a wine (yes, wine geeks do use "nose" as a verb) may be the most important step in the tasting process. The aromas in wine are fascinatingly wide-ranging: Hundreds of esters, aldehydes, and other compounds produced during fermentation create smells that take us well beyond the realm of crushed grapes.

An enology professor at the University of California-Davis, Ann Noble, created the now-famous Wine Aroma Wheel in the 1980s, an exhaustive compilation of the fruit-, earth-, wood-, and fermentation-derived aromas one might discover in a glass of wine. These aromatic markers are tells for someone attempting to identify a wine without looking at its label, but for the casual wine-lover, they are a way to organize wines in your mind and determine your tastes.

Here are three things to consider when assessing aroma: (a) lay off the cologne/perfume, (b) use a stemmed glass (to facilitate swirling, which volatilizes aromatic compounds), and (c) mind the temperature (too cold and you won't smell much; too hot and you'll get more alcohol "burn"). I'd suggest 50 to 55 degrees for whites (40 is refrigerator temperature) and 60 to 65 degrees for most reds.

Color Cheat Sheets by Variety

Popular grape varieties and where they fall on the color spectrum.

● WHITE GRAPES

Riesling	Straw/Silver/Green
Grüner Veltliner	Straw/Silver/Green
Albariño	Pale Yellow/Green
Sauvignon Blanc	Yellow/Gold
Chenin Blanc	Medium Gold
Pinot Gris/Grigio	Yellow/Gold/Copper
Chardonnay/ Viognier	Deep Yellow/Gold

● RED GRAPES

Sangiovese	Pale/Medium Garnet
Nebbiolo	Medium Garnet/Brick Orange
Pinot Noir	Cherry Red/Ruby Highlights
Grenache	Cherry Red
Tempranillo	Light/Medium Ruby
Merlot	Deep Ruby/Garnet/Magenta
Zinfandel	Deep Ruby/Garnet
Cabernet	Dark Ruby/Purple/Black
Syrah	Dark Ruby/Purple/Black
Malbec	Dark Ruby/Purple/Black
Aglianico	Dark Ruby/Purple/Black

Take your glass, give it a swirl, and smell the wine; there is no need to sniff like a bloodhound, just exhale first and breathe in gently. The aromas will fall into the following categories.

PRIMARY AROMAS

These are grape- and earth-derived scents: the apples, the citrus, the cherries, the herbs, the minerals. You'll learn to associate certain fruit characteristics with certain grape varieties and regions. Is that green apple or yellow apple? Or, more broadly, is it melon or citrus? When I think of Sauvignon Blanc from the Loire Valley in France, for example, I think grapefruit; with German Riesling, it's white peach; with Cabernet Sauvignon, cassis and black-currant. In addition to pinpointing which fruits you smell, how ripe are they? Is it a white peach that needs a few days on the counter before it's ready to eat, or is it juicy and bruised, or even stewed?

Then there are other naturally derived aromas of herbs, vegetables, flowers, spices, stones, and soil. Cabernet Franc, for example, has a characteristic note of bell pepper. Wines grown in limestone soils (like Champagne) often have a distinct chalkiness. Burgundian Pinot Noir combines bright red cherry fruit with a note of underbrush/forest floor. Grapes (and thus wines) pick up scents that reflect their natural environment. Just look at French Muscadet and Spanish Albariño, two whites that are grown close to the Atlantic coast and typically have a "sea spray" character. Lots of Mediterranean wines display herbal notes because of all of the nearby fragrant scrub (sage, rosemary, lavender).

As you become more closely acquainted with different varieties and regions and their telltale aromas, you'll be scanning store shelves with a much clearer idea of what to look for—or avoid—based on your personal preferences.

SECONDARY AROMAS

These are the aromas derived from fermentation and aging. Compounds produced during fermentation lend "perfume," while yeast-derived aromas—more notice- able in whites that have been left in contact with their lees—manifest as cream or rising bread dough. Wines aged in barrels, especially newer barrels with more abundant sugars and wood tannins, display notes of vanilla and buttered toast (in whites) and toffee/choco- late/smoke (in reds).

TERTIARY AROMAS

These aromas arise from age; the interaction between oxygen and the compounds in the wine over time alter the wine's chemical composition. Not all wines will have them. They smell like dried fruits, flowers, and herbs—rather than fresh ones—and include non-fruit scents, such as leather, wet leaves, and tobacco (in reds) and honey, caramel, golden raisins, and hazelnuts (in whites).

FINDING FAULT

In addition to the lovely fruits, flowers, and other inviting scents you're taking in, you may encounter less pleasant aromas that signal flaws. Many of these flaws are the result of unchecked microbial activity in the winery, while others are the result of bad handling or storage. The most common flaws follow.

Oxidation

When a wine is exposed to too much oxygen, it becomes flat, dull, and excessively "brown" in its color and flavors. It may be that it was held too long past its prime, or that it had a faulty or dried-out cork (perhaps from being stored upright rather than on its side). Or it was simply left open too long. In whites and reds alike, the aromas of oxidation are reminiscent of walnuts, caramel, and overripe apple.

TCA or "Corked" Wine

TCA is an abbreviation for trichloranisole, a naturally occurring compound created by phenols interacting with chlorine, which is used to sanitize corks. It has a musty, wet-cardboard smell that is transferred to the wine, and the intensity of that mustiness can vary from barely detectible to downright dank. Tainted natural corks affect about 3 percent of wines worldwide, but the musty TCA smell can develop anywhere. It can infect an entire winery. It is not harmful to one's health, it just smells bad.

Brettanomyces, aka "Brett"

This "spoilage yeast" creates volatile aromatic compounds that most tasters find unpleasant: "Horse blanket," "sweaty saddle," and "Band-Aid" are a few of the descriptors. As with TCA, intensity levels (and one's own sensitivity/perception) vary. In lower concentrations, "Brett" comes off as a pleasing, rustic funkiness; at higher levels, the "barnyard" aspect can be overwhelming.

Volatile Acidity

Here again, it becomes a question of degrees. "VA" is caused by bacteria in wine creating acetic acid, which gives off a vinegar/nail polish smell. It is more likely to develop in red wines, as red wines are more exposed to oxygen—the catalyst—during fermentation. In lower concentrations, some tasters find that VA lends a perfumed, lifted quality to a wine.

Volatile Sulfur/Reduction

The struck-match/gunflint smell of sulfur, used as both an antimicrobial agent and a preservative, can be excessive. Sometimes it has a rotten egg intensity, but it is also an aroma that may "blow off" as a wine oxygenates. Wines made in a reductive (oxygen-starved) environment—like fresh whites fermented or aged in closed steel tanks—can exhibit volatile sulfur aromas when first opened, after which those aromas dissipate.

Heat/Light Damage

UV rays are harmful to a wine, which explains the dark glass bottles and dark cellars for storage. Generally, a light-damaged wine has a flat, washed-out aromatic profile. Wines exposed to extreme heat or to wide fluctuations in temperature will also smell and taste flat or, in more extreme cases, as if they've been cooked.

STEP THREE

Sip and Savor

Finally, it's time to sip. Sipping a small amount enables you to draw in some air through your lips and aerate the wine on your tongue. This stimulates aroma receptors in the back of your nasal cavity. I've witnessed aggressive "slurpers" in the wine trade, people who slosh the wine around like they're rinsing for the dental hygienist. This is (a) unnecessary and (b) disgusting. A more delicate intake of air, as you would when sipping hot soup, works perfectly.

Taste and touch senses are in operation now. Evaluate how the wine tastes and also how it feels. Over time, you will come to associate certain flavors and textures with specific grapes and/or regions of the world. Developing this taste memory association is the surest way to find what you want in a store or articulate to the sommelier what you'd like in a restaurant.

STYLING AND PROFILING

A wine's "taste profile" is relatively easy to assemble. Refer to the sommelier tasting grid. Ask yourself: What fruit flavors stand out to you? How intense are they? Do you detect any flavors (vanilla, toast) that may have been derived from aging in wood barrels? What other non-fruit aromas are there? Soon you'll be able to tell what you're drinking before seeing the label.

Sweetness, or a perception of sweetness, is one huge component of the flavor profile (depending on the wine, tannin and acidity are other major components). We detect sweetness on the tip of the tongue, and everyone's experience of sweetness is a little different. Many wine regions of the world have their own standards as to what constitutes "dry" wine, "sweet" wine, and the assorted "off-dry" or "semisweet" styles in between—usually by measuring grams of sugar per liter of liquid. Here are some generally accepted ranges:

► Dry: 0 to 10 grams/liter

► Off-Dry: 10 to 18 g/l

► Semisweet/Demi-Sec: 18 to 50 g/l

► Sweet: 50 to 120 g/l

► Very Sweet: more than 120 g/l

"Sweet" is a tricky wine word, not just because we all perceive sweetness differently but because many consumers have come to associate it with bad wines that have something to hide. But it's often those few grams of sugar that give the Cabernet you love its voluptuous texture. And in wines such as German Riesling, high levels of residual sugar are offset by refreshingly high levels of natural acidity, which can play tricks on your mind: It is viscous and sweet on the tip of the tongue but then "finishes" dry. This leads us to a wine's structure and the role it plays in taste perception.

STRUCTURAL DYNAMICS

Along with sweetness, the other main components of wine are acidity, tannin, alcohol, and body.

Acidity, a key structural component in wine, is mostly detected on the sides of the tongue and is distinguished from tannin and alcohol in that it ignites a salivary response. High-acid wines taste zippy, lively, lip-smacking.

Tannins, the phenolic compounds derived from grape skins and wood barrels, are felt more on the middle/back of the tongue and have more bitterness. At higher concentrations, they can leave you with a dried-out feeling in your mouth, as if you blotted your tongue with a towel. Over time, tannins bind together and soften as they interact with oxygen.

Alcohol and body are interrelated, as higher alcohol means higher levels of glycerol, which creates viscosity. But there are other factors that influence the body of a wine, including how much "extract" it contains; remember, there is actual solid matter in wine (especially red wine), which contributes to its perceived weight on the palate. When alcohol levels are at the higher end of the spectrum (greater than 15 percent), you'll notice some "heat" both in your nostrils and on the palate.

Wine really does "open up" when it is exposed to air, so with young wines especially, don't base your judgments solely on what it's like 30 seconds after you've opened it. Wine is alive inside the bottle, and oxygen will bind with compounds in the wine to volatize aromas and break down tannin molecules. It's amazing how some young wines blossom when allowed to sit for a moment in a glass or decanter; on the flipside, some very old wines may "fall apart" right before your eyes, losing both color and flavor vibrancy not long after being opened.

STEP FOUR

So, Whaddaya Think?

Keep track of what you like and don't like; jot down some notes. Was the wine high in acidity or low? Was there any oak influence? How tannic was it? Was it full-bodied or light? Earthy or fruity? But most important of all: Did you like it or not, and why?

DRINKING IN THE BALANCE

One of the more macro assessments you should make is whether all the wine's elements are in harmony or whether certain features (or flaws) dominate. Balance is a highly desirable quality in a wine, just as it is in other aspects of life. Does the acidity make your lips pucker or is it refreshing and bright? Is the wine tooth-rattlingly tannic or just a touch "grippy"? Is it all fruit and no earth? Excessively oaky? Too alcoholic? When a wine is young, its assorted components are more forceful—but if they're in balance, you can taste and feel it and envision them knitting together over time.

COMPLEXITY

Wine is more than 80 percent water, and yet its range of aromas, flavors, and textures is seemingly limitless. Some wines have a long, fragrant aftertaste, known as the finish, whereas others disappear from memory and taste buds once you've swallowed a sip. Sense memory is really the longest "finish" you can have, and sometimes wine puts that sort of impression in your frontal lobe.

COMMEMORATE YOUR EXPERIENCE

You should develop your own system—whether it's stars, grades, points, or emojis—that will help you remember the experience. Consider each wine using a pared-down version of the grid: (a) sight, (b) smell, (c) taste, (d) texture/ body. Where the wine falls on the overall "weight" scale is likely your first consideration, followed by your perception of sweetness, acidity, and tannin. In the end, your personal tastes will fall into broader categories that you need not break down in infinitesimal detail. This is supposed to be fun—occasionally, sommeliers forget that.

5

HANDLE
WINE LIKE A
SOMMELIER

The first sommeliers were the people in charge of the pack animals used to transport wine. In the 19th century, the term came to refer to butlers who oversaw wine cellars in aristocratic households, likely the first people to test wines for fitness using little silver cups attached to chains around their necks. Most modern-day sommeliers will tell you that being a restaurant wine steward still incorporates some of the work of both the pack animal and the butler, but as the hospitality industry has gotten more professionalized in the United States, sommelier has become a position to aspire to.

One of the aims of this book is to give you the tools to be the sommelier in your own home. First and foremost, it involves putting as much forethought and advance preparation into wine as you do food in terms of the context, occasion, menu, and service. Let's start with the basics.

WHAT IS A SOMMELIER?

When I first got into the restaurant business 25 years ago, most restaurants did not have sommeliers, and if they did, that person was often a waiter or bartender with an interest in wine. Even today, there isn't any degree required to be a sommelier. A typical workday for a restaurant sommelier is not so different from a day you might spend putting together a dinner party in your home. Yes, sometimes it might involve a trade tasting off-site or meetings with wine salespeople, but for the most part, it's unboxing wine deliveries that have arrived, stocking shelves and the bar with wine, adding or removing wines from the wine list, and perhaps conducting a staff education session. During service, the sommelier is interacting with guests, opening and serving bottles, polishing glassware, helping run food from time to time (if the chef has anything to say about it), and generally performing the duties of an attentive host.

Here are the overarching responsibilities of a sommelier:

- ▶ Studying wine in some capacity and having firsthand knowledge of the wines (and food) on a restaurant's list/menu
- ▶ Handling restaurant wine orders
- ▶ Keeping track of costs
- ▶ Receiving deliveries and organizing/overseeing wine storage
- ▶ Writing and maintaining the wine list
- ▶ Managing wine service while preventing theft and waste
- ▶ Educating the rest of the staff about the wines you serve
- ▶ Advising customers on wine choices and assisting with all facets of restaurant service

Many great sommeliers learned on the job, but today there are many means of obtaining formal certification through organizations such as the Wine & Spirit Education Trust (WSET) and the Court of Master Sommeliers.

Master sommeliers were relatively scarce when I passed the exam back in 2000, but lately there's been a huge surge of interest in pursuing this credential. I think it's a reflection of the United States becoming more sophisticated as a wine culture, and it has undoubtedly gotten a push from the release of the documentary film *SOMM* (2013). Becoming a master sommelier (MS) is a time-consuming (and expensive) journey that involves passing four sets of exams: First, an introductory exam; then one to become certified; another to become advanced; and a final one to achieve master status. To become a master, you must pass a notoriously difficult three-part exam in which the categories are theory, service, and blind tasting.

The "theory" portion of the MS exam covers the facts and figures of the wide world of wine—the grapes, the geography, the appellations, the science, and the laws.

The "service" portion involves a mock service in which the "customers" are master sommeliers. They pepper the candidate with questions about often-obscure wines while also evaluating the candidate's ability to open, pour, decant, and conduct wine service in a skillful, stylish, and professional manner.

Then there's the "blind tasting" portion of the exam, which gets the most attention and is the most difficult to pass. The candidates are given six wines to taste and have no information about them. Based on taste memory and knowledge of wine theory, they must correctly identify four of the six wines down to their vintage, grape variety, region or origin, and quality level—and all within a time limit.

If this all sounds a little fanatical, well, it is. To me, the best sommeliers are those who embrace the original, non-snobby meaning of another French word, *connoisseur* (derived from a verb meaning "to know"): They just want to know everything there is to know about this thing they love, and they want to share that knowledge with anyone who'll listen.

SPEAKING THE LANGUAGE

Like any other society of like-minded obsessives—music geeks, film buffs, sports junkies—sommeliers employ a lot of insider terminology and a fair amount of name-dropping. It's only natural to find this intimidating (or annoying), but it's not necessary to "talk the talk" to drink well in a restaurant. The best way to talk to a sommelier is to get them talking. Ask questions. Put the sommelier to work for you. Here are a few ways to maximize your restaurant wine service experience:

► **Don't be afraid to talk budget.** For the longest time, people worried that it was *déclassé* to name their price range. As someone who worked in restaurants, I can safely say that the sommelier LOVES it when you give a number. Otherwise, we're just pointing at things until we land on something that feels right. Establish a price range and you've immediately narrowed the focus and simplified the decision.

► **Look for themes.** Let's say the restaurant is Italian with a focus on the cuisine of southern Italy. It would stand to reason that southern Italian wines would be the category you'd want to focus on. From there, is there a section of the list where there's a preponderance of a certain kind of wine from a specific appellation or grape? There's a good chance these are the wines the sommelier is most excited about.

- ▶ Speak up. This may seem obvious, but it's important to give the sommelier some information to work with. What are you in the mood to drink? Even saying something such as "I'd like a nice, crisp white" or "I like bold reds" is a good start. Giving the sommelier a sense of the "scale" of the wine you'd like to drink—light, medium, or full-bodied—is extremely useful.

- ▶ Compare and contrast. One effective sommelier conversation starter is to mention a style or brand of wine you like and ask if there exists something comparable. Maybe you've come to like Pinot Noir a lot but you're in, say, a Greek restaurant with an all-Greek list. Use the sommelier's knowledge of his or her list to find something in your wheelhouse.

- ▶ Live a little. Which is to say, be open to experimentation. If you get a good vibe from the sommelier, don't be afraid to hand over the reins. Sommeliers live for this. Make it so they're the ones trying to impress you.

KEEP YOUR COOL

When it comes to serving wine, there's nothing we get more consistently wrong than temperature. Even in purportedly fancy restaurants, I'm shocked at how often white wines are served too cold (direct from the refrigerator at 40 degrees Fahrenheit) and red wines are served too hot (70 degrees and up). In my view, the ideal service temperature for almost all white wines is 50–55 degrees Fahrenheit, which means: Let them sit on the table after they've come out of the refrigerator. If you really like them colder, then bring on the ice bucket; this is still about what *you* like. Just keep in mind that colder temperatures will mute or mask the wine's aromas and flavors.

Conversely, a red wine's alcohol "heat" and tannic bite are both exaggerated at warmer temperatures. Its fruitier aromas and flavors are flattened and the wine can taste metallic, and feel much heavier, when it is too warm.

The ideal range for most red wines is 60 to 65 degrees, although some lighter, higher-acid reds are even better at 50 to 55, as the chill mutes some of the acidic tartness and brings the fruit/floral components to the fore.

As for sparkling wines and Champagne, the conventional wisdom has always been to serve them ice-cold (or, at most, refrigerator temperature). I would agree with this for lower-priced sparklers without the mineral/acid structure of great Champagne. But Champagne should generally be treated like a fine white wine: The legendary Champagne house Bollinger, for example, suggests service temperatures equivalent to 50 to 54 degrees.

POUR WITH PURPOSE

Learning how to confidently (and cleanly) open and serve a bottle of wine is a great thing to add to your entertaining repertoire. Obviously, there are all sorts of cool wine-opening gadgets to choose from out there, but it won't surprise you to learn that my preferred tool is the good old-fashioned "waiter's corkscrew," also known as a "wine key" (a convenient mutation of the name of its German inventor, Karl Wienke). To me, this all-in-one device is the most efficient and elegant wine-opening tool available.

Having opened thousands of bottles with this style of wine key, there are two features I feel are most critical: (a) the metal lever that folds out and grips the lip of the bottle should be long and hinged, so that the "worm"—the actual corkscrew—can be drilled down deep and pulled out in two stages; (b) the small knife used to cut the foil capsule on the bottle is better when smooth-edged, not serrated (the latter can cause ragged capsule cuts).

To open a bottle like a sommelier, take the small knife and place it under the glass collar on the bottle that separates the neck and the lip. Run the knife around that edge, trying not to spin the bottle (which will agitate any sediment) while getting a clean cut. Use the edge of the little knife to pry the piece of capsule off the top of the bottle, then carefully insert the worm at a slight angle into the top of the cork and drill down. Then attach the metal lever to the lip of the bottle and gently pull upward. If you have the two-stage style with a hinged lever, start by attaching the short section up to the hinge, pull the cork out slightly, then reattach the lever at its full length and remove the cork. Going in at an angle and using a key with a two-stage lever will help you avoid breaking corks, even in older wines.

As wines age—ideally on their sides, with the wine in the bottle touching the cork and keeping it moist—their corks can occasionally become fragile. Even a deftly handled waiter's corkscrew may be too blunt an instrument for this job, which is where another rather old-fashioned instrument, the two-pronged Ah-So opener, comes in. Rather than inserting a corkscrew down through the middle of the cork, an Ah-So has two metal prongs that essentially grip it from the sides. It takes some practice, but when you learn how to gently wriggle the two prongs down between the cork and the wall of the bottle, there's no better way to extract a wet, fragile cork.

Once you've got the bottle opened, the next question is whether it needs to be decanted or not. Decanting is the process of pouring an entire bottle into a separate vessel. In general, there are two reasons to decant a wine: it's a young wine, white or red, that would benefit from aeration;

or it's an old red wine that needs to be separated from its sediment before serving.

Although it's not necessary for a screw-cap Pinot Grigio on pizza night, I will say that decanting young wines is almost never a bad idea. This is not a meticulous style of decanting I'm talking about—although be careful, many young red wines contain sediment, too—but rather a straightforward, glug-glug-type pour into a vessel with a wider mouth than a wine bottle. It need not be a fancy wine decanter, because the main objective is to aerate the wine to enhance its aromatics and soften/broaden its texture. This aeration starts with the action of pouring the wine and continues as it sits in the decanter.

With older red wines that are likely to have substantial sediment, there's a little more advance preparation involved. First, stand the bottle upright a day or two before you open it, so the sediment has a chance to settle at the bottom. After you've carefully extracted the cork, gently raise the bottle to the decanter and pour slowly, avoiding "glugging," until you see the sediment start to collect in the "shoulder" of the bottle. Sommeliers usually decant older wines over a candle or some light so they can see the creep of sediment and stop pouring before dumping any sludge in the decanter.

And finally, there's the pour. Sommeliers typically pour from the guest's right, with the label of the bottle facing the guest. Every effort is made to serve "openhanded," meaning you're moving around the table and facing each guest rather than reaching across, or "backhanding," them.

Bordeaux Varieties

Burgundy

White Wines

<u>The</u> <u>Right</u> <u>Glass</u>

You may be wondering, where's the gadgetry fun? For me, glassware is at the top of that list.

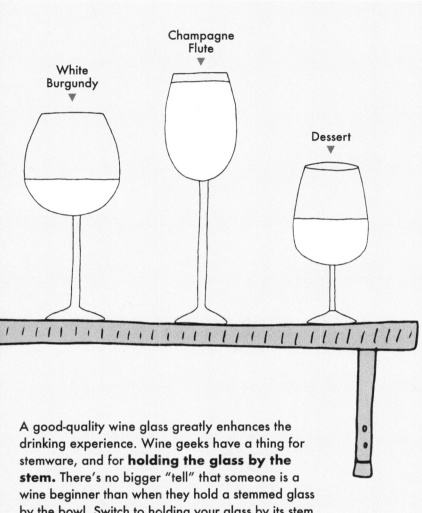

White
Burgundy

Champagne
Flute

Dessert

A good-quality wine glass greatly enhances the drinking experience. Wine geeks have a thing for stemware, and for **holding the glass by the stem.** There's no bigger "tell" that someone is a wine beginner than when they hold a stemmed glass by the bowl. Switch to holding your glass by its stem (and, perhaps, mastering "the swirl") and you'll enhance your wine credibility exponentially.

As for the glasses themselves, one of the main features of a good wine glass is a relatively thin, smooth, "cut" rim, as opposed to a glass with a "beaded" rim that leads to dribbling. Overall, you'll experience a smoother delivery of the wine to your palate in the thinnest-walled glass you can afford.

The reason wine glasses have traditionally had stems is because of the desire to sip wine without having its temperature altered by your hands. Indeed, the only time you'd want to hold a glass by the bowl is when you need to warm it up because it was served too cold.

White wine glasses tend to be smaller than red wine glasses because whites are traditionally served chilled; they maintain their chill better when there is less surface area of wine exposed to the surrounding atmosphere. Larger red wine glasses allow for more interaction of wine with oxygen, which helps break down tannin molecules and soften the bite of the wine. In both cases, wine glasses are never meant to be filled all the way to the rim, but instead should have plenty of room for the liquid to be swirled around without spilling. This aeration process is critical: As aromatic esters in the wine interact with oxygen in the air, they are "volatilized," meaning they jump from the glass into your smell/taste receptors.

As for Champagne "flutes," their narrow design is meant to slow the escape of CO_2 gas after the wine has been poured, so the wine maintains its effervescence. If you aspire to serve an assortment of different wines in one sitting, stock the following:

6–12
Champagne flutes

6–12
white wine glasses
of 14 to16 ounce capacity

6–12
red wine bowls
or "Burgundy" glasses
of 20+ ounces capacity
(these are the rounder bowls
with the narrower opening
at the top; best for lighter,
aromatic reds like Pinot Noir
because they trap aromatic
compounds within the bowl)

6–12
"Bordeaux"
red wine glasses
of 20+ ounces capacity
(these are taller with a wider
opening; for fuller-bodied
reds like Bordeaux or Brunello
di Montalcino, which
benefit from more contact
with surface oxygen)

STORE IT AWAY, DRINK IT ANOTHER DAY

The vast majority of wines made in the world are meant to be enjoyed either immediately or within a few years of their release. But there may come a time, if you've got the space and the means, when you'd like to "lay some wine down" for future enjoyment. If so, here are the basics of storing wine:

▶ **Standard cellar temperature is 55 degrees Fahrenheit.**
This is the "just right" point between too hot and too cold.

▶ **Keep temperatures constant.**
In addition to guarding against wines getting too hot or too cold, it's equally important to prevent temperature swings.

▶ **Turn lights out.**
Excessive exposure to light can alter the chemistry in the bottle and produce off flavors.

▶ **Store bottles on their sides.**
This keeps corks moist while also providing the most efficient use of available space.

WHAT TO DO WITH OPEN BOTTLES?

Although there is a lot of good wine preservation technology out there, much of it involving the use of an inert gas to keep oxygen away, I also think most open bottles, especially good bottles, can be recorked, put in the refrigerator, and revisited up to three days later without any significant decline in quality. This would not apply to long-aged wines, but with younger wines you'll find many to be even more enjoyable on day two. Fuller-bodied reds especially can be open for several days before showing the ill effects of too much oxygen exposure, and putting them in the refrigerator slows the oxidation process down significantly. Don't wait too long, but don't fret if you don't finish a whole bottle in one sitting. It's got quite a long way to go before it is vinegar.

THROW A BLIND TASTING PARTY!

Tasting wines "blind" is an enlightening, often humbling, way to learn about wine once you have a little bit of "sighted" practice in hand. There's no more objective way of evaluating a wine and assessing its quality than by tasting it without looking at its label or knowing what it costs.

Blind tasting is valuable for establishing benchmarks, as is comparison tasting. If you were to taste six wines from the same region or grape without any information about their producer or price, you'd likely be surprised by the results. Only by tasting lots of Chablis, for example, can you establish what you consider to be a quality benchmark for Chablis. The exercise of blind tasting is not just about assessing character traits, but also about assessing *value*. This is especially important to a wine professional seeking to put the very best example of X on their wine list, but it's also important to anyone seeking perspective on what's worth the money and what isn't.

Consider hosting a blind-tasting party. Everyone brings a wine they like, with the bottle concealed. Each guest pours wine for the group members, who then make their assessments as to what it could be. Using all their powers of deduction and drawing on everything they know about color, aroma, flavor, and texture, not to mention the tastes of other people in the group, everyone competes for the title.

The Well-Equipped Wine Pantry

If space permits, an assortment of wine glasses of different shapes and sizes is always useful for entertaining. But if you're in the market for one all-purpose glass that can handle anything, I'd suggest something with a capacity of no less than 16 ounces (to accommodate swirling) and with a taller, less bulbous shape. Here are two elegantly styled all-purpose glasses at opposite ends of the price spectrum, along with a few other tools you'll need for proper sommelier-style wine service:

» **All-purpose glass #1:** The budget-friendly Libbey Signature Kentfield Estate 4-piece All-Purpose Glass Set will only set you back around $35.

» **All-purpose glass #2:** If you feel the urge to splurge, nothing makes wine taste better than when it's sipped out of an elegant stem. Zalto is setting the bar with its Denk'Art Universal. Each stem retails for around $60.

» **The waiter's corkscrew:** Of all the gadget wine openers on the market, the trusted waiter's corkscrew is really the only tool you need. A double hinge for long cork extraction is helpful, and you can easily find a good one for under $20.

» **The all-purpose decanter beloved by sommeliers:** The very simple and affordable Riedel Cabernet Sauvignon Decanter is as close to the all-purpose decanter as I have found; it works for everything at $69.

» **The best stopper for sparklers:** The best way to keep unfinished sparkling wine fresh with bubbles is to use a classic champagne stopper, readily available for under $10.

The vineyard perched atop the rolling hills of Tuscany at Tenuta Sette Cieli.

6

WINE AROUND THE WORLD

While many factors influence a wine's style, climate is undoubtedly the most impactful. Around the globe, grapevines flourish between 30 to 50 degrees of latitude in the Northern and Southern Hemispheres. In general, cooler-climate wines tend to be lighter in body, with crisper fruit flavors and lower alcohol. Warm or hot areas usually produce wines with more body, riper fruit flavors, and higher alcohol. Thirteen countries produce most of the wines we see on the market, and they're grouped in two main categories: "Old World," which refers to historic wine nations in Europe, and "New World," which includes everywhere else.

■ ■ FRANCE

France ranks at or near the top in total wine production, and it has shaped wine culture. Much of our shared wine language is French, including the concept of *terroir,* which describes the "total natural environment" of a wine: the climate, soil, altitude, orientation, and other attributes of the vineyard(s) from which it hails. French and other Old World wines are usually labeled with a place name first. Here are the key regions:

Bordeaux is named for a city along the Garonne River in southwestern France. Situated near the Atlantic coast, it is France's most prolific wine region, known for manicured *châteaux* and vines rooted in clay, sand, and alluvial (i.e., river-borne) gravel. The Atlantic tempers the climate and provides a long growing season. Cabernet Sauvignon, Cabernet Franc, and Merlot are the key red varieties, while Sauvignon Blanc and Sémillon drive white wine production.

The heart of Bordeaux is where the Dordogne and Garonne Rivers meet and become the Gironde. On the western bank of the Gironde (the "Médoc"), where soils are richer in gravel, Cabernet Sauvignon thrives in iconic towns like Margaux, Saint-Julien, Pauillac, and Saint-Estèphe. Bordeaux wines are usually blends. On the east bank, in appellations such as Saint-Émilion and Pomerol, where soil is clay-dominant, Merlot and Cabernet Franc take center stage. Bordeaux reds are powerful expressions of black and red fruits, herbs, graphite, and tobacco; they're some of the longest-aging wines money can buy.

The top white wine zones are Graves, Pessac-Léognan, Sauternes, and Barsac. Graves and Pessac produce exotically fruited dry whites from Sauvignon Blanc and Sémillon. Those same varieties are used in sweet nectars from appellations such as Sauternes and Barsac. Here, grapes shrivel on the vine and become sugar-rich through the action of a mold known as Botrytis cinerea.

Burgundy stretches from Dijon to Lyon, with vineyards on limestone/clay slopes west of the Saône River. To the northwest of Dijon is Chablis, while to the south, approaching Lyon, is Beaujolais, where the region's signature red grape, Pinot Noir, gives way to its juicier, ruby-hued cousin, Gamay.

Burgundy's cool continental climate produces the world's most acclaimed Pinot Noirs and Chardonnays in vineyards first cultivated by Cistercian monks a thousand years ago. This monastic influence still reigns in that it is the most carefully mapped-out wine region on earth, divided into singular vineyard sites, or *crus*. "Grand Cru" ("great growth") and "Premier Cru" ("first growth") are the highest rankings given to top-performing vineyards.

Burgundy is known for "varietal" wines containing 100 percent of the chosen grape. Chardonnays range from the zesty, mineral (and usually unoaked) wines of Chablis to more substantial, barrel-fermented styles in villages further south. The heartland of Burgundy is called the *Côte d'Or* ("Golden Slope"), which is broken into two sections: the northerly Côte de Nuits, where Pinot Noir dominates in places like Gevrey-Chambertin and Vosne-Romanée; and the Côte de Beaune, where Chardonnay shines brightest in Puligny-Montrachet, Meursault, and Chassagne-Montrachet.

The Pinot Noirs display energy and aromatic complexity thanks to the cool climate and limestone soils. The mix of power and finesse in these reds is legendary, but be warned: This benchmark Pinot Noir experience does not come

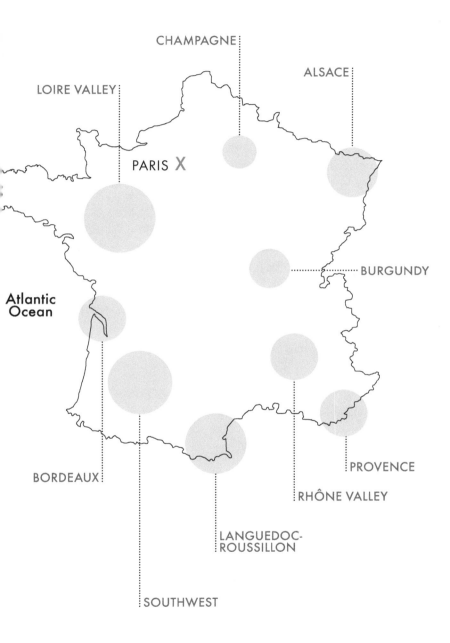

CHAMPAGNE

ALSACE

LOIRE VALLEY

PARIS X

Atlantic
Ocean

BURGUNDY

BORDEAUX

PROVENCE

RHÔNE VALLEY

LANGUEDOC-
ROUSSILLON

SOUTHWEST

cheap. Generally produced on a smaller scale, Burgundies are some of the world's most treasured collectibles.

For more affordable red Burgundy, look to Beaujolais, where Gamay grows in soils of granite and schist. Although perhaps best known for raw, grapey, nouveau wines bottled immediately after harvest, there's much more to Beaujolais: Focus on reds from the 10 *cru* villages, such as Morgon, Fleurie, and Moulin-à-Vent; these wines have complexity and structure to rival the Pinot Noirs of their neighbors at a fraction of the price.

Champagne is on the 49th parallel, near Europe's northern limit for viticulture (although, due to climate change, the line is moving). The soils are chalky limestone. Perhaps more than any other region, Champagne demonstrates how powerful place names can be. Its producers remind us that "all Champagne is sparkling wine, but not all sparkling wine is Champagne."

Loire Valley, in north-central France, follows the 600-mile Loire River to the Atlantic Ocean. The climate is relatively cool at this latitude, while soils vary. In the famous inner Loire villages of Sancerre and Pouilly-Fumé, known for crystalline, mineral Sauvignon Blancs (and ethereal reds from Pinot Noir), soils mix clay, limestone, and flint.

The central Loire regions of Touraine and Anjou-Saumur have alluvial sand/gravel mixed with clay and yellowish limestone called *tuffeau*. The varietal focus shifts to Chenin Blanc for whites (Vouvray and Savennières) and Cabernet Franc for reds (Chinon, Bourgueil, Saumur). Chenin Blanc is a chameleon, with high acidity and a distinctive quince/apple fruit character in wines ranging from bone-dry to sweet to sparkling. Loire Cabernet Francs are spicier, tobacco-scented, and lighter bodied than their Bordeaux counterparts.

At the mouth of the Loire are the Muscadet appellations, in mostly sandy/granitic soils around the city of Nantes. Muscadet is a hybrid grape/place name for whites made from the Melon de Bourgogne variety; these bracingly fresh wines have a touch of Atlantic "sea spray," as well as creaminess from being bottled *sur lie* (on their lees or spent yeasts).

Rhône Valley is south of Burgundy, following the Rhône River down to the Mediterranean Sea. Its northern and southern sections are tied together by the river, yet they have different climates. The moderate continental climate in the north supports Syrah, which thrives in granitic soils and offers a mix of black/blue fruits, peppercorn, and smoked meat, along with lifted acidity and minerality. Côte-Rôtie, Saint-Joseph, and Hermitage are the top Syrah appellations.

The southern Rhône is a warmer Mediterranean climate known mostly for reds driven by the berry-fruited, herbal Grenache grape. The wines are often blended and include a good amount of Syrah and Mourvèdre. Châteauneuf-du-Pape is the red-wine king of the southern Rhône, but look also for luscious, less expensive analogs from Gigondas and Vacqueyras.

■ ■ ITALY

Among the world's largest producers, Italy may have the most diverse wine landscape, with varying climates and soils, and a staggering variety of native grapes. Each of Italy's 20 administrative regions has its own specialties and in some cases a specific grape or wine is found only in a single province or two. This is both the challenge and the attraction of Italian wine. Much of Italy is warm and Mediterranean, although there are exceptions.

Piedmont is one of these exceptions, in the northwest corner of Italy, ringed by Alps. The cool, continental climate is not dissimilar to Burgundy's, and its most famous wines, Barolo and Barbaresco reds from the Nebbiolo grape, are often compared to red Burgundies. They can be both elegant and intense, with rose-petal aromas, red fruits, leather, and powerful tannins. Notes of mushroom and truffle develop with aging, which Nebbiolo does beautifully.

But Piedmont is more than Nebbiolo. It is really a wine nation unto itself, world-famous for wines such as Asti Spumante, a sparkling (and delicately sweet) wine produced from the Moscato grape. The crisp white wines of Gavi, made in chalky soils in Piedmont's southeast corner, are compared to Chablis. And the Barbera and Dolcetto grapes, "second bananas" to the noble Nebbiolo, produce deliciously affordable alternatives to expensive Barolos. Hyper-local specialties abound here, including featherweight, spicy reds from varieties such as Grignolino and Pelaverga.

Friuli-Venezia-Giulia, in the extreme northeast, has become Italy's most distinguished white wine region. Positioned at a cultural crossroads, with Austria to the north and Slovenia/Croatia to the east, the region's varietal bottlings

LOMBARDY

IEDMONT

TRENTINO-ALTO ADIGE

VALLE
AOSTA

VENETO

FRIULI-VENEZIA GIULIA

MILAN
VENICE

EMILIA-ROMAGNA

LIGURIA

LE MARCHE

ABRUZZO

ROME
X

SARDINIA

CAMPANIA

UMBRIA

APULIA

BASILICATA

TUSCANY

CALABRIA

SICILY

include mineral whites from the Friulano grape. Other specialties include the taut, citrusy Ribolla Gialla and a number of "French" grapes, especially Sauvignon Blanc. Pinot Grigio, with unique weight, richness, and fruit concentration, is another Friulian white to seek out, as are the region's distinctive "orange" wines, which are made from white grapes left in contact with their skins during fermentation.

Tuscany is the homeland of Sangiovese, which reaches its apex in the central Tuscan wines of Chianti Classico, Vino Nobile di Montepulciano, and Brunello di Montalcino. In Chianti Classico, between Florence and Siena, the climate is continental and the soil is a rocky mix of marl and sandstone, creating tart reds with black cherry fruit and a woodland savor. Montepulciano and Montalcino are similar, although the latter feels like a Mediterranean influence. Brunello di Montalcino, the only one of the "big three" comprising 100 percent Sangiovese, is also the most powerful, dark-fruited wine of the group, with perhaps the greatest potential for aging.

Tuscany also has a long Mediterranean coastline, which, in addition to producing herbaceous, sea-kissed whites from the Vermentino grape, is the birthplace of "super-Tuscan" blends such as Sassicaia and Ornellaia. These opulent reds gained international fame for giving an Italian voice to Bordeaux grapes such as Cabernet Sauvignon and Merlot, which adapted well to the maritime climate of the region.

Campania is an ancient cradle of viticulture, originally a Greek outpost and later home to Roman agricultural writers like Pliny the Elder. Campania has a warm climate and lots of volcanic soils, which have proven hospitable not just to the beefy, smoky Aglianico grape but to some of Italy's more distinguished white varieties: Fiano, Falanghina, and Greco. Fiano has a floral, slightly honeyed profile as grown in the inland area of Avellino, while Greco, in its most famous incarnation, Greco di Tufo, takes on a stony minerality imparted by the volcanic tuff (*tufo*) it grows in.

Campania is home to the Taurasi DOCG, an appellation in the Apennine foothills nicknamed the "Barolo of the South" for its powerful Aglianico-based reds. These are tannic, smoky reds with a pronounced black fruit/tobacco character.

Sicily once produced mostly bulk wines, but today it is not merely prolific but one of Italy's most dynamic regions, thanks in large part to the wines of Mount Etna, Europe's largest active volcano. This unique growing zone is at a very southerly latitude but boasts some of the highest-elevation vineyards in Europe. The main white grape of Etna is the racy, appley Carricante, while Etna Rosso is driven by the elegant, brightly fruited Nerello Mascalese. This Etnean specialty has a more Pinot Noir–like character than the other signature red of Sicily, Nero d'Avola, which is more purple-fruited and richer in body.

🏳️ SPAIN

Spain, while among the top three Old World wine producers, is also enjoying a modern wine renaissance. Most of
central and southern Spain is warm and Mediterranean,
while some iconic regions in the north are on high plateaus
near mountain ranges, where the climate has an arid,
high-desert feel. In the northwestern region of Galicia, you
find a lusher, greener Spain, with cooler, wetter climates for
salty coastal whites and lively, spicy reds.

Rioja is probably Spain's best-known wine region, well
north of Madrid. Following the Ebro River, Rioja's climate is
continental with wide temperature disparities; altitude also
plays a role. The best soils are clay, limestone, and sandstone
found at higher elevations. The softly contoured Tempranillo
grape is the principal variety and is often blended with
Garnacha (Grenache) in long-lived red wines. Healthy doses
of oak buttress red fruits, wet earth, leather, and structured
tannins. Rioja is also a noteworthy producer of full-bodied
whites, the best ones based on the aromatic Viura grape.

Ribera del Duero is south of Rioja and hugs the Douro
River as it flows westward. It is warm with large diurnal
temperature swings. The soil is sandier near the river, with
more clay and limestone at higher elevations. The region
produces only red wine and some rosé, with most vineyards dedicated to Tinto Fino (Tempranillo). The wines here
are not usually as elegant as Rioja but are more dense and
powerful. Darker fruit flavors are common, with notes of
tobacco, meat, mocha, and turned earth.

Priorat produces dark, concentrated, dry reds from
Garnacha and Cariñena (Carignan). The region sits atop a
bluff in Catalonia, a short distance from the Mediterranean,
and is known for its black, fractured-slate soils.

Galicia is the region in northwestern Spain that includes appellations such as Rías Baixas, Ribeiro, and Ribeira Sacra. It is best known for salty, peach-scented whites from the Albariño grape, and buoyant, dark-fruited reds from Mencía. These wines currently have the ear of oenophiles.

Penedès, in Catalonia in the northeast, is responsible for Cava, a sparkling wine. These vineyards grow near a Mediterranean coastal range outside Barcelona. The wines are produced in the classic Méthode Champenoise but are sold at prices well below those of Champagne.

CASTILLA Y LEÓN

GALICIA

Bay of Biscay

RIOJA & NAVARRA

BARCELONA

MADRID X

Atlantic Ocean

CATALONIA

SOUTHEAST SPAIN

ANDALUCÍA

▣ PORTUGAL

The Douro Valley in northern Portugal is one of the world's oldest "delimited" wine zones. It is famous for Port wines—rich, fortified reds—that were floated down the Douro and shipped to the world from the coastal city of Porto. This is an arid, often blazingly hot valley with terraced vineyards carved from schist. These days, much of the focus has shifted to dry, red table wines made from the same grapes that once went into Port.

Vinho Verde is a regional as well as stylistic name (translated as "green wine"). It is on the northwest coast and is influenced by the Atlantic. Vinho Verde produces fresh, lively white wines from grapes such as Loureiro, Trajadura, and Alvarinho (Albariño), and is marked by low alcohol and a slight effervescence.

Douro, as noted above, is extremely rugged, becoming hotter as you move inland from the Atlantic. This is Port country, and though the wines are mostly blended, the purple-fruited, broodingly tannic Touriga Nacional grape dominates both fortified and dry reds.

Dão is another region with dry reds of noteworthy structure. It sits below the Douro and is enclosed by mountains, making it a warmer Mediterranean climate. Many indigenous grapes grow in Dão but, again, Touriga Nacional produces the top wines.

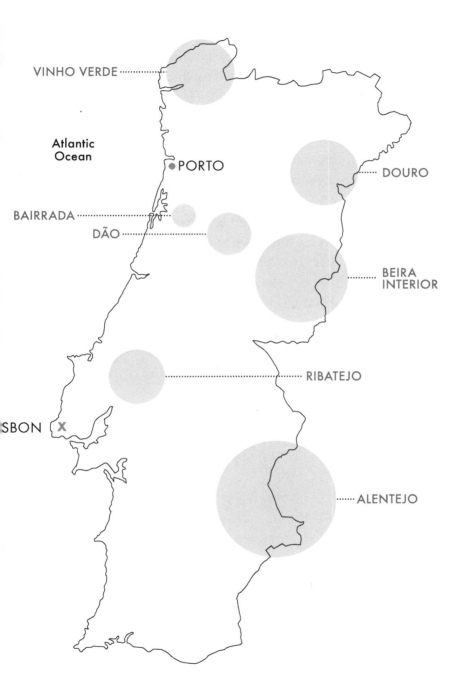

VINHO VERDE

Atlantic
Ocean

•PORTO

DOURO

BAIRRADA

DÃO

BEIRA
INTERIOR

RIBATEJO

SBON X

ALENTEJO

≡ AUSTRIA

Winemaking has existed in Austria for thousands of years, and its striking vineyards are now best known for bone-dry, unoaked white wines. The main wine regions are nestled around the Danube River on the eastern side of the country, known as Niederösterreich ("lower Austria"). The climate is cool and continental with cold winters and warm summers. Vineyards overlooking the Danube can be extremely steep and terraced, requiring manual farming. The primary grapes are Grüner Veltliner and Riesling, producing mineral-etched wines that leave your mouth watering. Reds from this region are usually lighter in style and include some uniquely peppery, dark-fruited wines from the local Zweigelt and Blaufränkisch grapes. Austrian Spätburgunder (Pinot Noir) has a willowy, woodsy feel and is continuing to improve in quality and recognition.

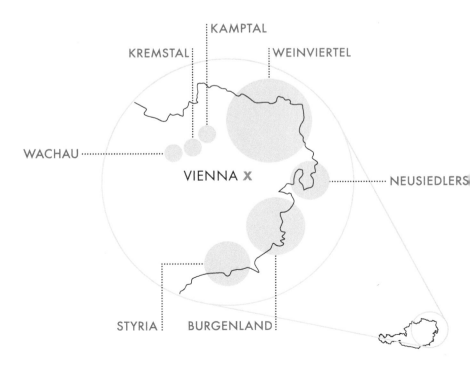

KAMPTAL

KREMSTAL

WEINVIERTEL

WACHAU

VIENNA x

NEUSIEDLERS

STYRIA

BURGENLAND

🏴 GERMANY

Germany's wine regions are clustered in its southwest, along the Rhine River and its tributaries. Some of
Germany's wine zones are among the coolest in Europe.
German wine laws are complex, and many people are
under the misimpression that German wines (Riesling
especially) are all sweet. The reality is that Riesling is
produced in myriad styles, from bone-dry to sweet to
sparkling. Riesling accounts for nearly one-quarter of all
plantings in Germany: It is a durable, late-ripening grape
that can handle the colder climate, and when made well,
can produce some of the most captivating wines on earth.

Mosel is a river valley with some of the coldest, steep-
est, most northerly vineyards in Europe. The region
is known for blue, slate soil, which helps with heat
retention. Ripeness is a challenge, so Mosel wines tend

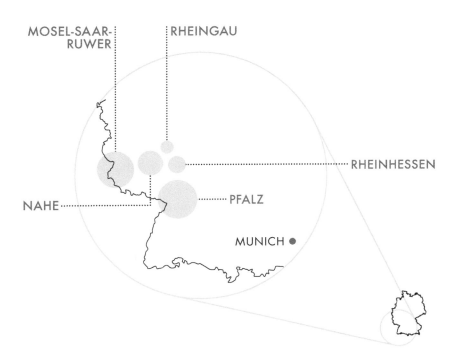

to be off-dry/sweeter styles with low alcohol, balanced by refreshingly crisp acidity.

Rheingau, southeast of Mosel on the Rhine, is the oldest wine region in Germany. Vineyards all face south and the upper vineyards are known for slate soil. The wines are riper, with more stone fruit flavors. Dry wines are more common.

Pfalz is farther south, bordering Alsace, France. The soil mixes limestone, sandstone, red slate, and alluvial gravel. The climate is sunny and dry, ultimately a bit warmer, with wine styles skewing dry.

🇬🇷 GREECE

Greece is an up-and-coming Old World region. Much of the climate is Mediterranean, but there are some mountainous regions of the north with more continental conditions. Greece has many unique indigenous grapes, but consumers are just now becoming familiar with them.

Nemea is a top red wine region. It is attached by a small land bridge to the country's mainland and is located just a couple hours south of Athens by car. The best red grapes are Agiorgitiko and Xinomavro. Agiorgitiko (a.k.a. St. George) produces bright, exotically spicy red wines.

Macedonia is completely landlocked and stretches across the northern part of the country. Xinomavro can reach incredible quality levels here, producing powerful earthy reds with dark fruit, chocolate, and firm tannins.

Santorini is possibly the world's greatest wine tourist destination, combining ocean views and magical sunsets with bright, fresh white wines made from Assyrtiko. This white grape has been cultivated on the island for thousands of years.

MACEDONIA

Aegean Sea

SAMOS

ATHENS

Mediterranean
Sea

Sea of
Crete

SANTORINI

PELOPONNESE
Nemea

🇺🇸 UNITED STATES

CALIFORNIA

While wine is produced in all 50 states, California has led the way for New World American wines since the late 1970s. It took a long time for America's wine industry to rebound from Prohibition, but the "Judgment of Paris" in 1976 propelled California wine into the spotlight: Two American wines scored higher than several French wines in a blind tasting. The world was stunned, and in a country once dominated by spirits and beer, wine had officially arrived.

Napa Valley is generally dry and Mediterranean with large diurnal temperature shifts. The valley is greatly influenced by the fog that comes up from the San Pablo Bay and the Pacific to cool the grapes at night, causing them to retain their acids. Altitude and vineyard orientation play a large role, with wines from hillside appellations like Howell Mountain and Mount Veeder showing more firm and mineral structure. Chardonnay and Sauvignon Blanc are the leading white varieties. Napa Chardonnay is known to be rich, buttery, and oaky, though that has shifted a bit in recent years. On the red side, the region is best known for rich, dark, fruit-driven Cabernet Sauvignon, Merlot, and Pinot Noir in the cooler subregion of Carneros. Zinfandel, which is nearly exclusive to California, is also grown in the warmer areas.

Sonoma County is west of Napa and is cooler and more coastal in nature. Similar to Napa, altitude plays a significant role in viticulture, as does the oceanic fog that rolls in by way of the Petaluma Gap. Both the white and red grape varieties of this region are similar to Napa's.

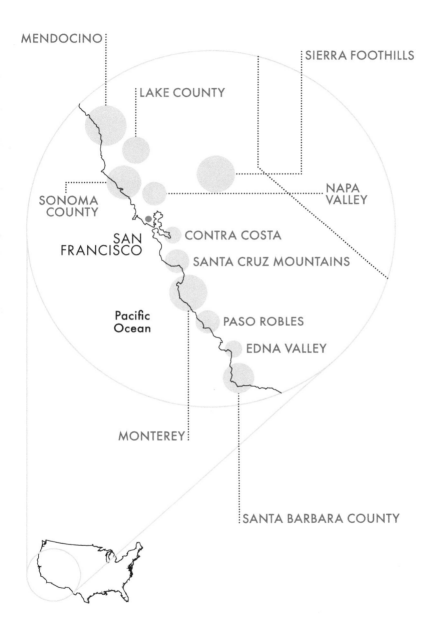

MENDOCINO

LAKE COUNTY

SIERRA FOOTHILLS

SONOMA
COUNTY

NAPA
VALLEY

SAN
FRANCISCO

CONTRA COSTA

SANTA CRUZ MOUNTAINS

Pacific
Ocean

PASO ROBLES

EDNA VALLEY

MONTEREY

SANTA BARBARA COUNTY

WASHINGTON STATE

Washington State winemaking happens mostly east of the Cascade Mountains, where the climate is hot and desertlike. Huge diurnal temperature shifts throughout the growing season help keep grapes fresh. Because the region averages fewer than 10 inches of rain per year, vineyards source from the Columbia, Snake, and Yakima Rivers. While quality white wines are produced from the Chardonnay and Riesling varieties in Washington, red wine is the main focus. The three primary reds include Cabernet Sauvignon, Merlot, and, especially, Syrah, which can be reminiscent of wine in some areas of the Northern Rhône.

OREGON

In just the last 40 years, Oregon's Willamette Valley has gone from being mostly unpopulated and unknown for wine to one of the world's great Pinot Noir destinations. Still, the wines are relative steals compared to other benchmark Pinot Noirs. A few breaks in the coastal range separating Willamette Valley from the Pacific Ocean allow cool air to funnel through, but the region is protected from excessive rain and is situated at one of the more northerly latitudes in the United States. As this region continues to evolve, more distinct subregions are emerging, boasting an ever-growing number of great producers.

NEW YORK STATE

New York is the third-largest wine-producing state in the United States. Climates vary greatly based on the subregions, but the white wines from the cooler, continental Finger Lakes have garnered well-deserved attention recently. Look for world-class expressions of dry Riesling.

CHILE

Influenced early by the Spanish, Chilean wine now has a decidedly French bent, both in terms of grapes planted and winemaking styles. Many vines were brought over from Bordeaux in the late 1800s, when Chileans often built estates in a style reminiscent of Bordelais *châteaux*.

The Chilean climate varies widely based on north/south orientation. The Andes, which run the length of the country, set a spectacular backdrop for the wine-producing regions, and the ice melt from those mountains provides natural irrigation for the vineyards. The Humboldt current that comes up from Antarctica regulates temperatures, bringing icy waters, cool air, and fog.

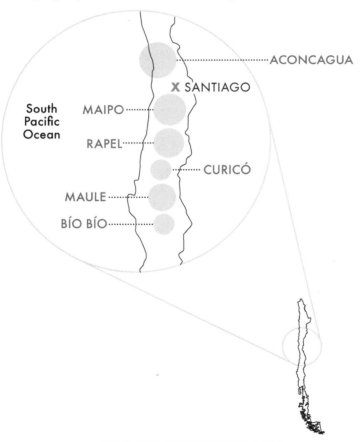

A perfectly
ripened cluster of
Cabernet Franc.

Aconcagua and Valle Central (Central Valley) are the top producing regions in Chile. The smaller Aconcagua is known for unoaked Chardonnay, Pinot Noir, and crisp, grassy Sauvignon Blanc. Dominated by red Bordeaux varieties, the Central Valley produces more than 80 percent of Chile's wines. The Maipo and Colchagua Valleys are the most widely known subregions, producing Cabernet Sauvignons, Bordeaux-style blends, and herbaceous, elegant reds from the country's signature grape, Carmenère, thought to be a lost Bordeaux variety from epochs past.

ARGENTINA

Much of the historical wine production in Argentina bore the influence of Spanish and Italian immigrants, but like Chile, most high-quality wines are produced from "French" grapes. Argentine wine country is arid, residing in the eastern rain shadow of the Andes. Due to the warmer climate, irrigation with Andes snowmelt is critical. Altitude is key to maintaining acidity, though grapes achieve high sugar levels from warmth and intense luminosity. The average vineyard elevation is 3,000 feet, which allows for ripening by day and cooling by night.

The popularity of Argentine wines grew quickly at the turn of the 21st century, with reds from the inky, tannic Malbec grape leading the way. Argentina has also had success with Cabernet Sauvignon, Chardonnay, and the aromatic white Torrontés.

Mendoza is the largest viticultural area in Argentina and the modern home of the Malbec grape. Historically, Malbec was found in Bordeaux and nearby Cahors. Malbec from Argentina has a distinct purple color, violet aromas, ripe dark fruits, spice, and notes of turned earth. The more polished tannins of Argentine Malbecs offer new perspective to consumers accustomed to the rugged, funky wines of Cahors.

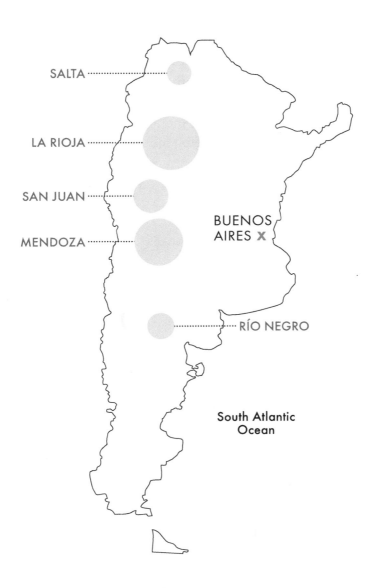

SALTA

LA RIOJA

SAN JUAN

MENDOZA

BUENOS AIRES X

RÍO NEGRO

South Atlantic Ocean

🏴 SOUTH AFRICA

South Africa's wine regions are mostly coastal. The climate is considered maritime and is widely regulated by the Benguela, an oceanic current coming up from Antarctica. Chenin Blanc (a.k.a. Steen) dominates white grape plantings, but quality levels vary and production is declining. The Stellenbosch appellation is known for zippy, mineral-driven Sauvignon Blanc as well as Cabernet Sauvignon–based reds. In addition to recent success with the Bordeaux varieties, richer Shiraz/Syrah wines are becoming more popular. The signature South African red is Pinotage, a smoky, savory, full-bodied crossing of Pinot Noir and Cinsault. Farther south, the Walker Bay district in the Western Cape is looking stronger in Chardonnay and Pinot Noir production.

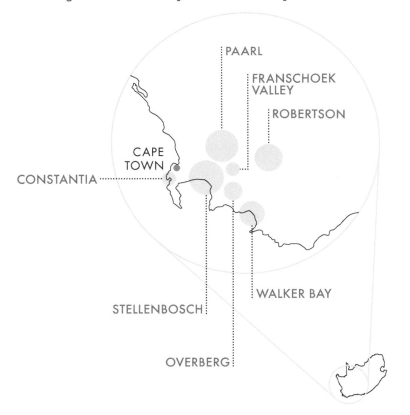

PAARL

FRANSCHOEK VALLEY

ROBERTSON

CAPE TOWN

CONSTANTIA

WALKER BAY

STELLENBOSCH

OVERBERG

▓▓ NEW ZEALAND

New Zealand has the southernmost wine regions in the world. Parts of the country can be warm and maritime, but several subregions are cooler, particularly on the South Island, where vineyards reach toward the South Pole. Overall, quality has skyrocketed in the past 30 years. New Zealand built its reputation around bold, pungent Sauvignon Blancs in the 1990s, but since that time, Pinot Noir has been gaining momentum. Under the radar are crisp, high-acid Chardonnays, which can be particularly compelling.

AUCKLAND

Tasman Sea

GISBORNE

HAWKE'S BAY

NELSON

MARLBOROUGH

WAIRARAPA

X

WELLINGTON

WAIPARA
CANTERBURY

South Pacific Ocean

CENTRAL OTAGO

Marlborough is a cool, dry region on the South Island known for Sauvignon Blanc. In fact, Marlborough produces most of New Zealand's wine. The Sauvignon Blancs have an herbaceous quality with intense flavors of tropical fruits and ripe citrus.

Central Otago is an up-and-coming South Island region known for energetic, aromatic Pinot Noir from relatively high-elevation vineyards. Well-draining schist soils and a cool climate produce wines that compete with the best of the New (and Old) World.

🇦🇺 AUSTRALIA

Australian wine had its moment in the United States a while back. This New World region is generally hot and dry, with most of the quality wine regions scattered along the southern coast. South Australian regions are cooler, but can easily achieve ripeness and intensity. Australia produces a wide and high-quality assortment of whites and reds, but Shiraz (Syrah) is the grape that has driven international success. Notable cultivated white grapes include Riesling, Sémillon, Viognier, and Chardonnay. Other red grapes include Grenache and Cabernet Sauvignon.

Barossa is north of Adelaide in South Australia and known for more of a Mediterranean climate. This is one area the phylloxera louse (an aphid that infested vineyards in the late 1800s and ruined a huge swath of the world's wine grapes) never reached and many of its vines are more than 100 years old. Reds from Shiraz, Grenache, and Cabernet Sauvignon rule this region and are densely concentrated, with dark fruits, herbal notes, smoked meat, spices, and chocolatey tannins.

Clare Valley is a continental climate north of Barossa, known for Shiraz and Cabernet Sauvignon. Riesling, however, has become the star, producing compellingly fresh, bone-dry, high-acid wines with notes of lime blossom and wet stone.

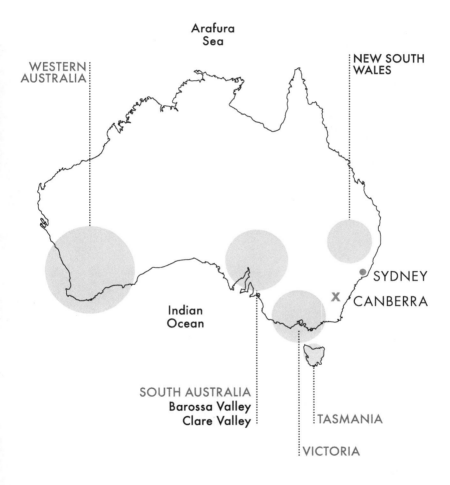

Wine Far and Wide

It's been said that a rising tide lifts all boats, and when it comes to wine, the baseline quality level worldwide has never been higher. As technology and investment finds its way into "new" corners of the wine world, places not widely known for their wines—some of them among the most historic wine-producing regions of the world—are attracting attention.

Probably the most noteworthy of these is the former Soviet republic of Georgia, in the Caucasus, which is considered the ancient birthplace of *vitis vinifera* grapes and winemaking. Very traditional styles of wine, including "orange" whites from native grapes, some of them fermented in old clay amphorae, have become better recognized among wine cognoscenti.

Ex-Yugoslavian regions like Slovenia, Croatia, and Bosnia-Herzegovina are producing some beautiful Adriatic-influenced whites from grapes like Malvasia, as well as some bold, tangy reds.

There are many far-flung wine regions that will deliver value and interest for your wine dollar these days: Baja, California (Mexico); Texas Hill Country (United States); Okanagan Valley, British Columbia (Canada); Great Britain (where a sparkling wine culture has blossomed); Canary Islands (Spain); Tokaji (Hungary); and many more.

7

PAIRING WINE WITH FOOD

To take your "home sommelier" game to the next level, think of wine as food. The most skilled sommeliers are the ones whose mission it is to improve a meal with wine. After all, wine is meant to be consumed as food and paired *with* food. As you learn more about wine, you will begin to intuit which wines best enhance what you are eating. A sommelier works in close cooperation with the chef, and if those two people are one in the same (i.e., you), then all the better.

You may have encountered the countless articles outlining the "rules" of food-wine pairings. My experience has made me realize that because of the many variables to consider, there shouldn't be hard and fast rules. It's a little bit art and a little bit science, with some cultural literacy thrown in for color. Here's some of what I've learned over the years.

SALT, FAT, ACID, HEAT

With a hat tip to *New York Times* bestselling author Samin Nosrat, I submit that her "elements of good cooking" are also essential to devising a successful wine pairing. Consider the following:

Salt tends to exaggerate the effects of tannin and/or alcohol and vice versa. So pairing a salty dish with a tannic/alcoholic wine will make the dish saltier and the wine sharper and "hotter." Crisp, fresh white wines tend to pair better with salty/briny items like oysters or prosciutto.

Fat in food, be it the marbling of a rib-eye steak or the saturated fat in cheese, is most effectively broken down by acidity and tannin in wine. They work in concert: Acid foils fat (picture how grease in a sink full of water dissipates if you squeeze in a drop or two of lemon juice) and fat acts as a palate cleanser of sorts, absorbing tannins and softening their bite. One of the greatest wine/food marriages of all time is a racy, high-acid Loire Valley Sauvignon Blanc, such as Sancerre, with the region's rich, sticky goat's-milk cheese, Crottin de Chavignol.

Acid not only cuts through fat; acid also works with acid. Acidic wines pair best with dishes that themselves contain a lot of acidity, like vinaigrettes, lemon butters, and citrus.

Heat from chilies or other hot spices exaggerates alcohol burn and tannic bite, making wines taste metallic and the spice taste spicier. Approach with caution and an off-dry white or a light-bodied, softly contoured red.

A STUDY IN CONTRASTS
AND FINDING COMMON GROUND

Food and wine pairings are often presented as a choice between complementary or contrasting, when they might end up being both. In a contrasting pairing, it's not contrasting flavors you're looking for, but contrasting textures—as in the acid/tannin versus fat example on page 125. A tannic Italian Barolo paired with a rich, fatty beef braise is textural contrast at its best, as the wine cleanses the palate of fat with each sip. Champagne is a terrific partner for cheese thanks to the "scrubbing bubble" effect of its effervescence. And off-dry German Riesling is magic with spicy Thai, Cantonese, and other five-alarm dishes, as its subtle residual sugar and slight viscosity help tame the heat.

There are also instances when the wine offers aromas and flavors that complement similar ones in a dish. It may be the earthiness of mushrooms, the bloody, mineral tang of raw beef, or, on the white side, a buttery slab of chicken or fish in need of a creamy, oak-aged white.

A QUESTION OF SCALE

Matching the overall "scale" of the dish—light, medium, rich—with a wine of comparable scale is one major consideration. Although I've enjoyed pairing light, high-acid reds with richer meat dishes, almost as a means of relief and refreshment, it generally pays to keep the matchup in the same weight class. Picture a dish of poached halibut and green vegetables with a crisp, unoaked white, or a slab of porterhouse steak with a bold Napa Valley Cabernet Sauvignon.

CONSIDER THE WHOLE PLATE

The centerpiece protein on the plate doesn't always drive the pairing. Sometimes it's the side or sauce that really defines the dish. When I think of steak au poivre, for example, versus a more simply prepared steak, I might hold back on the tannin/alcohol levels a bit, given all that black pepper: maybe a Beaujolais or medium-bodied Syrah instead of a full-throttle Cabernet?

MODULATING SWEETNESS

Desserts are the hardest dishes to pair with wine. A very sweet dessert paired with a dry wine often causes the wine to taste dry to the point of puckering unpleasantness. Conversely, a fully sweet dessert wine paired with a similarly sugary dessert can be cloying. Many of the classic sweet wines of the world were conceived as desserts unto themselves, or as the sweetening element in a dessert. Sweet wines (Port most famously) also provide luxurious contrast to salty, funky cheeses such as Stilton. Nuttier, more oxidative "fortified" wines, such as Madeira or Sherry, whether dry or moderately sweet, can be exceptional for desserts incorporating chocolate and nuts.

PLACE-SPECIFIC PAIRINGS

There's an old saying you hear a lot in the wine business: "If it grows together, it goes together." A home sommelier could prepare a regional recipe and pair it with an iconic wine of that region. It could be as simple a pairing as Loire Valley Muscadet with Atlantic oysters, or something more detailed, like a fresh Provençal rosé paired with bouillabaisse.

What's on the Plate and What to Pair It With

To start your wine adventure, here is a basic guide of classic food and wine pairings.

Cheese

Fresh/ Goat (*Chèvre*)	Loire Valley Sauvignon Blanc; dry Riesling
Bloomy Rind (Camembert, Brie)	Chablis (*Chardonnay*); Pinot Bianco
Washed Rind (Epoisses, Taleggio)	Alsatian Gewürztraminer; Vouvray (*Chenin Blanc*); crisp mountain whites from Savoie; Italian Alps
Blue/Veined (Stilton, Gorgonzola)	Port; Sauternes; Vin Santo; sweet Rieslings
Hard (Parmigiano, Manchego)	Medium-bodied, low tannin reds (*Rioja, Chianti*); richer whites (*Chardonnay*); Sherries

Vegetables

Salads/ Vinaigrettes	Sauvignon Blanc; Austrian Grüner Veltliner
Green Vegetables	Grüner Veltliner; German Riesling
Mushrooms	Aged white Burgundies (*Chardonnay*); earthy reds (*Italian Nebbiolo, Burgundy Pinot Noir*); oxidative Sherries such as Amontillado
Root Vegetables	Oak-aged whites from Chardonnay; Marsanne/Roussanne (*Rhône, France*); white Rioja (*Spain*)

Meats

Chicken	Oak-aged Chardonnay (*Burgundy, California*); Pinot Noir (*German/ Oregon*); Gamay (*Beaujolais*)
Pork	Alsatian whites; German Riesling; Chardonnay; lighter reds (*Pinot Noir, Spanish Tempranillo*)
Beef	Bordeaux reds; Californian/ Chilean/Washington Cabernet Sauvignon; Argentine Malbec; Italian Sangiovese (*Brunello di Montalcino*); and Nebbiolo (*Barolo*)
Lamb	French Syrah (*Côte-Rôtie, Saint-Joseph*); Mediterranean reds (*Bandol Rouge, Châteauneuf-du- Pape, Cannonau di Sardegna*); California Zinfandel
Duck/ Other Game	Deeper Spanish reds (*Ribera del Duero, Priorat*); Italian Barbera; Cabernet Sauvignon; Italian Sangiovese (*Chianti Classico*)
Sausages	Alsatian and German Rieslings; Jura (*France*) reds; Italian Barbera/Dolcetto

Fish/Shellfish

Oysters/ Clams	Loire Valley (France) Muscadet; Champagne/Cava
Octopus	Spanish Albariño; Portuguese Vinho Verde; Chenin Blanc
Sole/ Halibut/ Branzino	Italian whites (Pinot Grigio, Verdicchio, Vermentino); unoaked Burgundy whites such as Chablis (Chardonnay)
Swordfish	Richer "island" whites from Sicily, Sardinia, Santorini
Shellfish Stews	Provençal rosés and whites (Bandol Blanc); Italian Vermentino (Liguria)
Salmon	Oregon Pinot Noir; Gamay from Beaujolais (France)
Tuna	Pinot Noir; Gamay
Sardines/ Mackerel	High-acid, low-fruit whites such as Spanish Txakolina or Fino Sherry; Champagne

Herbs/Spices

Parsley/ Oregano	Vermentino (Italy, Southern France); Grüner Veltliner
Cilantro/ Basil/Mint	Sauvignon Blanc (California, New Zealand)
Rosemary	Loire Valley Cabernet Franc (Chinon); Merlot
Nutmeg/ Baking Spices	Oak-aged Chardonnay
Paprika	Mencía (Galicia, Spain); Blaufränkisch (Austria)
Lavender/ Juniper	Syrah/Shiraz; Mourvèdre
Black Pepper	Syrah/Shiraz; Cabernet Sauvignon

Dessert

Chocolate Cake	Madeira; Port; Brachetto d'Acqui (*Piedmont, Italy*)
Fruit Pies/ Clafoutis	Off-dry German Riesling; Tawny Port
Cheesecake	Sauternes and Barsac (*Bordeaux*); oxidative Sherries (*Oloroso*)
Biscotti/ Cookies	Italian Vin Santo; Passito di Pantelleria
Almond/ Hazelnut/ Pecan	Vin Santo; sweet Sherries (*Oloroso, Pedro Ximénez*)

CONCLUSION

SO YOU'RE A SOMMELIER NOW. WHAT'S NEXT?

While sommelier certification may not be your mission, you can still put all of your studies here to great use. When all is said and done, the best way to learn about wine is to taste. Then taste some more. Experimenting, comparing and contrasting, and being open-minded are the keys to defining what you like.

At home, your goal should be to elevate your everyday wine experiences. If you enjoy tackling new recipes in the kitchen, consider the wine pairing—not as an afterthought, but as a key ingredient that can add much to the meal. For me, being a good sommelier is not just what to drink but also how and why: What's the occasion? What's the menu? Who's on the guest list?

As I noted earlier, the baseline level of wine quality worldwide is at an all-time high, so experimentation carries far less risk than it may once have. Truly "fine" wine need not necessarily be expensive. Maybe at one time you needed to be rich to be a wine connoisseur, but not anymore. Now, all you need to be is game. When you travel, try to visit wineries and vineyards. When you're in a restaurant or retail store, ask questions and give those professionals a chance to shine.

Most of all, trust your own palate. Accumulating knowledge and experience is great, but your ultimate goal is to find wine you like to drink. So happy hunting, and cheers!

RESOURCES

Bastianich, Joseph, and David Lynch. *Vino Italiano: The Regional Wines of Italy*. New York: Clarkson Potter, 2005.

D'Agata, Ian. *Native Wine Grapes of Italy*. Berkeley University of California Press, 2014.

Dharmadhikari, Murli. "Composition of Grapes." Iowa State University. Accessed October 8, 2019. https://www.extension.iastate.edu /wine/files/page/files/compositionofgrapes.pdf.

Eisenman, Lum. "Wine Clarification and Stabilization." Genco Winemakers. Accessed October 8, 2019. http://www.gencowinemakers .com/docs/Wine Clarification and Stabilization.pdf.

Goode, Jamie. "The Visual Assessment of Wine." GuildSomm. Accessed October 8, 2019. https://www.guildsomm.com/public_content/features/ articles/b/jamie_goode/posts/the-visual-assessment-of-wine.

"The Great White South: An Introduction to Châteauneuf-Du-Pape Blanc." Vinography.Com: A Wine Blog. Accessed September 9, 2019. http://www.vinography.com/archives/2014/08/the_great_white _south.html.

"How to Manage Pests." UC IPM Online. Accessed October 8, 2019. http://ipm.ucanr.edu/PMG/PESTNOTES/pn7481.html.

Johnson, Hugh, and James Halliday. *The Vitner's Art: How Great Wines Are Made*. New York: Simon & Schuster, 1992.

"The Key Chemicals in Red Wine—Colour, Flavour, and Potential Health Benefits." Compound Interest, February 18, 2017. https://www.compoundchem.com/2014/05/28/redwinechemicals/.

MacNeil, Karen. *The Wine Bible*. New York: Workman Publishing, 2015.

Margalit, Yair. *Winery Technology & Operations: A Handbook for Small Wineries*. San Francisco: Wine Appreciation Guild, 2011.

Markoski, Melissa M., Juliano Garavaglia, Aline Oliveira, Jessica Olivaes, and Aline Marcadenti. "Molecular Properties of Red Wine Compounds and Cardiometabolic Benefits." *Nutrition and Metabolic Insights* 9 (August 2016): 51–57. doi:10.4137/NMI.S32909.

McKirdy, Tim, and Danielle Grinberg. "The Differences Between Primary, Secondary, and Tertiary Aromas, Explained." VinePair, June 18, 2019. https://vinepair.com/articles/wine-aromas-explained.

Meadows, Allen D. *The Pearl of the Côte: The Great Wines of Vosne-Romaneé*. Winnetka Burghound Books, 2010.

Napa Valley Vintners. "The Life Cycle of a Grape." Napa Valley Vintners. Accessed October 8, 2019. https://napavintners.com/napa_valley/life_cycle_of_a_grape.asp.

Parr, Rajat, and Jordan Mackay. *Secrets of the Sommeliers: How to Think and Drink like the World's Top Wine Professionals*. Berkeley Ten Speed Press, 2010.

Parr, Rajat, Jordan Mackay, and Joe Woodhouse. *The Sommeliers Atlas of Taste: A Field Guide to the Great Wines of Europe*. Berkeley Ten Speed Press, 2018.

Puckette, Madeline, and Justin Hammack. *Wine Folly: The Essential Guide to Wine*. New York: Avery, 2015.

Reinagel, Monica. "Myths about Sulfites and Wine." *Scientific American*, July 15, 2017. https://www.scientificamerican.com/article/myths-about-sulfites-and-wine.

Robinson, Jancis. *The Oxford Companion to Wine*. Oxford: Oxford University Press, 2015.

Steadman, Ralph. *Untrodden Grapes*. Orlando, FL: Harcourt, 2005.

"Sulfites in Wine: The Facts." The Organic Wine Company. Accessed October 8, 2019. http://theorganicwinecompany.com/sulfites-in-wine-facts.

White, Kelli. "The Sweet Spot: Understanding Sugar in Wine." GuildSomm. Accessed October 8, 2019. https://www.guildsomm.com/public_content/features/articles/b/kelli-white/posts/understanding-sugar-in-wine.

Zraly, Kevin. *Windows on the World Complete Wine Course*. New York: Sterling Epicure, 2018.

INDEX

A

Acidity, 30–31, 64–65, 67
Aconcagua (region), 114
Aging, 12, 78
Alcohol by volume (abv), 32, 67
Amarone, 50
Ancestral Method, 38–39
Anthocyanins, 6
Antioxidants, 30
Appellations, 22
Argentina, 114–115
Argentine Malbec, 51
Aroma, 59, 62–65
Australia, 118–119
Australian Shiraz, 51
Austria, 104

B

Bacteria, 12
Balance, 33
Barolo, 50
Barossa (region), 118–119
Barsac, 52
Bâtonnage, 12
Beaujolais, 47
Biodynamics, 20
Blends, 18
Blind tasting, 86
Body, 29, 33, 67
Bordeaux (region), 91–93
Bordeaux Blanc, 43–44
Bordeaux Cabernet
    Sauvignon, 50–51
Botrytis, 52
Bottling, 13, 17
Brettanomyces ("Brett"), 64
Brunello di Montalcino, 50
Burgundy (region), 92–93

C

California, 108–109
California Chardonnay, 43
California Pinot Noir, 48
California Sauvignon Blanc, 42–43
California sparklers, 40
Calories, 20
Campania (region), 97–99
"Cap" of skins, 7–10
Carbon dioxide (CO_2), 7, 37
Cava, 40
Central Otago (region), 117–118
Chablis, 42
Champagne, 39, 77
Champagne (region), 93–94
Champagne Rosé, 45–46
Châteauneuf-du-Pape, 51
Châteauneuf-du-Pape Blanc, 43
Chemical compounds, 7, 20
Chile, 111, 114
Citric acid, 31, 33
Clare Valley, 118–119
Cold stabilization, 13, 31
Color, 57–58
Condrieu, 44
Connoisseurs, 75
Copper sulfate, 17
"Corked" wine, 64
Corks, 77–78
Crémant, 40
Crushing, 6, 17

D

Dão (region), 102–103
Decanting, 78–79
Demi-Sec, 38
Denominations of origin, 22
Dessert wines, 51–52

Destemming, 6
Diacetyl, 31
Disgorgement, 37
Dosage, 37, 38
Douro (region), 102–103
Doux, 38
Dryness, 37

E

Effervescence, 37
Eiswein, 52
Ethanol, 7, 32
Evaluation, 68–69

F

Fermentation, 6–11, 12, 17
Field blends, 18
Filtration, 13
Fining, 13
Finish, 69
Flaws, 63–65
Food pairings
    cheese, 131
    dessert, 136
    fish/shellfish, 134
    herbs/spices, 135
    meats, 133
    overview, 125–127
    vegetables, 132
Fortified wines, 51–53
France, 91–95
Franciacorta, 40
Free-run juice, 11
Friulano, 43
Friuli-Venezia-Giulia (region), 96–98
Fruit tannin, 29–30, 33

G

Galicia (region), 101
Galician Red Wine, 47
Gavi, 42
Georgia (country), 120
German Riesling, 45
Germany, 105–106

Gewürztraminer, 44
Glassware, 80–83, 87
Grapes
    color, 57–58, 60–61
    crushing, 6
    harvesting, 3–5
    ideal climate for growing, 90
    vineyard lifecycle, 14–16
Greece, 106–107
"Green apple" acidity, 31
The grid, 56. See also Evaluation;
    Sight; Smell; Taste
Grüner Veltliner, 41–42

H

Harvesting, 3–5, 16, 17
Heat damage, 65

I

Intensity, 57–58
Italy, 96–99

J

Jura Reds, 47

L

Labels, 21–23, 32
Lees, 12
"Legs," 59
Light damage, 65
Liqueur de tirage, 37
Liqueur d'expédition, 32
Loire Valley, 93–95
Loire Valley Cabernet Franc, 48
Loire Valley Chenin Blanc, 42
Loire Valley Sauvignon
    Blanc, 41

M

Macedonia, 106–107
Maceration, 6, 30
Malic acid, 31
Malolactic conversion, 31
Malolactic fermentation, 12

Marlborough (region), 117–118
"Master sommeliers" (MS), 74–75
Mendoza (region), 114–115
Metabolization, 6–7
Moscato d'Asti, 52
Mosel (region), 105–106
Muscadet, 41

N

Napa Valley, 108–109
Napa Valley Cabernet
    Sauvignon, 50–51
Natural wine, 19–20
Nebbiolo Rosato, 46
Nemea (region), 106–107
"New World" wines, 22. See also
    Argentina; Australia; Chile;
    New Zealand; South Africa;
    United States
New York (state), 110
New Zealand, 117–118
New Zealand Sauvignon Blanc, 45
Noble, Ann, 59
Northern Rhône Syrah, 48
"Nosing," 59. See also Smell
Nosrat, Samin, 125

O

"Old World" wines, 21, 25. See also
    Austria; France; Germany;
    Greece; Italy; Portugal; Spain
Opening bottles, 77–78
"Orange" wine, 49, 120
Oregon, 110
Oregon Pinot Gris, 43
Organic viticulture, 21
Oxidation, 64
Oxygen, 7, 12

P

Pairing. See Food pairings
Penedès (region), 101
Pétillant-Naturel, 40
Pfalz (region), 105–106

Piedmont (region), 96–97
Pinot Noir Rosé, 46
Port, 52
Portugal, 102–103
Pouring, 79
Pressing, 6, 11–12
Press wine, 11
Primary aromas, 62–63
Priorat (region), 100–101
Prosecco, 41
Provence, 46

R

Racking, 11, 12
Red Burgundy, 46–47
Reduction, 65
Red wines. See also Dessert wines;
    Rosé wines
    color, 58, 61
    fermentation, 7–10
    full-bodied, 50–51
    glassware, 81–83
    ideal temperature, 46, 48, 77
    light-bodied, 46–47
    medium-bodied, 47–48
    pressing, 11–12
Residual sugar, 11, 32
Resveratrol, 30
Rheingau (region), 105–106
Rhône Valley, 93, 95
Ribera del Duero (region), 100–101
Rioja (region), 100–101
Rioja Blanco, 44, 48
Rosé wines, 45–46

S

Sangiovese, 48
Santorini (region), 106–107
Sauternes, 52
Secondary aromas, 63
Sediment, 78–79
Sekt, 40
Sherry, 53
Sicily, 97, 99

Sight, 57–59
Smell, 59, 62–65
Sommeliers, 72–76
Sonoma County, 108–109
South Africa, 116
Spain, 100–101
Sparkling wines, 37–42, 77
Steiner, Rudolf, 21
Stoppers, 87
Storage, 84
Sugar, 6, 11, 37
Sulfites, 17–18
Sulfur dioxide (SO_2), 12, 17
Sweetness, 32, 37, 66–67, 127

T

Tank/Charmat Method, 38
Tannins, 6, 29–30, 33, 67
Tartaric acid, 30–31
Taste, 65–68
TCA (trichloranisole), 64
"Tears," 59
Temperature
    fermentation, 10–11
    serving, 76–77
    storage, 84
Terroir, 21, 91
Tertiary aromas, 63
Texture spectrum, 29
Torrontés, 45
Traditional/Champagne Method
    (Méthode Champenoise), 37
Tuscany, 97–98

U

United States, 108–110

V

Valle Central (Central Valley), 114
Varietal wines, 18
Vineyard lifecycle, 14–16
Vinho Verde, 42, 102–103
Vin Santo, 52
Viscosity, 59
Volatile acidity (VA), 64–65
Volatile sulfur, 65

W

Waiter's corkscrews, 77–78, 87
Washington (state), 110
Washington State reds, 51
White wines. See also Dessert wines;
    "Orange" wine; Sparkling wines
    aromatic, 44–45
    color, 57–58, 61
    fermentation, 10
    full-bodied, 43–44
    glassware, 81–83
    ideal temperature, 41, 77
    light-bodied, 41–42
    medium-bodied, 42–43
    racking, 11
Wienke, Karl, 77
Willamette Valley Pinot Noir, 47
Wine keys, 77–78
Wood, 12
Wood tannin, 29

Y

Yeast, 6–7, 32, 64

Z

Zinfandel, 50

ACKNOWLEDGMENTS

WRITING A BOOK IS A REAL LABOR OF LOVE, both more challenging and rewarding than anticipated.

Throughout this process, there was never enough time and certainly not enough space for everything I wanted to say. Honestly, organizing this first-time effort was harder than a flight of six wines blind.

Despite these varied constraints, I've been blessed with a great group of supporters who have helped me get this book across the finish line.

To my amazing, endlessly patient partner, Maria, and our beautiful son, Alessandro, I give heartfelt thanks for your unwavering support. Our Alessandro, who at age three was forced to sacrifice a great deal as I missed birthday parties, holidays, and the first day of school . . . Okay, it wasn't as bad as all that, but there were many nights we did not share a bedtime story, as I was writing a story of my own.

To my business partner, mentor, and dear friend, Marilyn Scripps. You have afforded me the opportunities of a lifetime, shared with me countless bottles of legendary wine, and supported me in every aspect of my life for 20 years. Your love and generosity have been pillars to my success. Thank you.

I also want to thank two individuals who were incredible resources when it came to the actual writing of this book: To Jeanne Stiles, who has worked with me for nearly 10 years and has always been my confidential sounding board, this book would not have been as good without you. And to David Lynch, my longtime close friend and colleague—and the author of my favorite wine book, *Vino Italiano*—your inspiration and expertise were paramount to the completion of this book.

To my UNLV Professor Donald Bell, who helped me discover that I could, quite possibly, make a career out of this wine thing: I am truly humbled and forever grateful for the insightful direction you generously offered me. I can only imagine the inspiration and guidance you have given to countless students, and the positive impact you've had on their lives, as well.

And, of course, a huge, arms together, hands clasped bow to my editor, Sean Newcott, who knew when to challenge me and made this a better read. To the entire team at Rockridge and Callisto, Amanda Kirk, Holly Haydash, Michael Hardgrove, and Caryn Abramowitz, thank you.

I learned so much writing this book, not the least of which was relearning and confirming a fundamental truth about what makes me tick: While I love everything about the endlessly compelling subject of wine, it is sharing the experience that brings true joy.

The steeped terraced
vineyards of Tenuta
Sette Cieli.

PHOTOGRAPHY ACKNOWLEDGMENT

THE BEAUTIFUL PHOTOGRAPHS FEATURED throughout this book capture the magic of Tenuta Sette Cieli in Tuscany, Italy—a stunning, organically farmed winery perched on a 1,300-foot hilltop with unobstructed views of the coastline and Tyrrhenian Sea.

The English translation is "The Estate of Seven Skies," a reference to the countless iterations of the sky when viewed at any time of day from the estate. The winery is famous for producing elegant Cabernet Sauvignon, Cabernet Franc, and Merlot from densely planted, hand-tended vineyards.

For me, Sette Cieli exemplifies the best of Italy: Breathtaking, terraced vineyards . . . painstaking attention to detail in the winery . . . standard-setting hospitality. Most importantly though—like any great winery—Sette Cieli's innate composition and culture are anchored by tremendously talented people.

Over the years, I've had the good fortune to spend many weeks with the Ratti family, and now Sette Cieli is like a second home. The Rattis' refinement, kindness, and generosity are further reflected in the profile of their delicious, complex wines!

ABOUT THE AUTHOR

Chicago-based master sommelier and serial entrepreneur **Ken Fredrickson** spent his early career working alongside culinary giants Wolfgang Puck and Charlie Trotter. After leaving the restaurant world, Ken built and sold innovative, customer-focused wine and spirits distribution companies and completed a winery turnaround. Currently, he is incubating a global spirits import group that owns several of its own brands, and he operates Tenzing, A Wine and Spirits Company, which is dedicated to the hospitality sector. An Ironman participant and enthusiast, Ken focuses his charitable efforts on the Mayo Clinic and its specific treatment of mood-related illness and bipolar disorder. Ken is a longtime supporter of Pilot Light Chefs program, an organization promoting nutrition through education in Chicago public schools. In his free time, Ken can be found entertaining friends and family, traveling with his partner, Maria, and chasing their four-year-old son around. Don't miss his wine adventures on Instagram @kenfredricksonms.

CPSIA information can be obtained
at www.ICGtesting.com
Printed in the USA
LVHW070353141219
640251LV00003BB/7/P